NORTH CAROLINA

·The· M ·Co·

NORTH CAROLINA

A STUDY IN

ENGLISH COLONIAL GOVERNMENT

BY

CHARLES LEE RAPER, Ph.D.

ASSOCIATE PROFESSOR OF ECONOMICS AND ASSOCIATE PROFESSOR OF HISTORY IN
THE UNIVERSITY OF NORTH CAROLINA

New York:

THE MACMILLAN COMPANY

LONDON: MACMILLAN & CO., Ltd.

1904

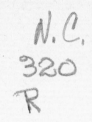
Press of
THE NEW ERA PRINTING COMPANY,
LANCASTER, PA.

To
H. F. W.

PREFACE.

As far as the author is aware, this is the first study from the original sources of the provincial government of North Carolina embracing the whole period, and from the point of view of England as well as that of the colony. Four of the ten chapters were published, in a very limited edition, during the year 1901, but in form of statement these have been changed in a decided manner. To Professor Herbert L. Osgood, of Columbia University, the author acknowledges his profound gratitude for assistance rendered in many ways. The kind assistance of Professors Kemp Plummer Battle, Henry Horace Williams and Edward Kidder Graham, of the University of North Carolina, in reading the manuscript and proof is also acknowledged.

CONTENTS.

CHAPTER I.

INTRODUCTION: A REVIEW OF THE PROPRIETARY PERIOD.

CHAPTER II.

THE GOVERNOR UNDER THE CROWN.

CHAPTER III.

THE COUNCIL UNDER THE CROWN.

CHAPTER IV.

THE LOWER HOUSE OF THE LEGISLATURE UNDER THE CROWN.

CHAPTER V.

THE TERRITORIAL SYSTEM AND ADMINISTRATION.

CHAPTER VI.

THE FISCAL SYSTEM AND ADMINISTRATION.

CHAPTER VII.

THE JUDICIAL SYSTEM AND ADMINISTRATION.

CHAPTER VIII.

THE SYSTEM OF DEFENCE.

CHAPTER IX.

THE CONFLICTS BETWEEN THE EXECUTIVE AND THE LOWER HOUSE UNDER THE CROWN.

CONTENTS

CHAPTER X.

THE DOWNFALL OF THE ROYAL GOVERNMENT.

CHAPTER I.

INTRODUCTION.

A REVIEW OF THE PROPRIETARY PERIOD.

THE life of one particular period in the development of a people, as of an individual, has a most intimate relation with that of former periods. The history and the development of North Carolina after 1729, when the crown assumed control of it, were, therefore, profoundly influenced by that of the proprietary period, which began with the year 1663; the economic, political and social forces of the earlier years of the colony's life continued on, to a very considerable extent, throughout the royal period. For this reason, therefore, it is necessary to consider at least the general outline of the development under the patentees. The details of their administration, so far as they pertain to land, finance, justice and defence, will receive due consideration under the chapters devoted, almost exclusively, to these subjects. Here it is necessary only to trace in outline and to discuss the general powers, duties and policies of the proprietors, with the effects of their administration.

Carolina, including what was afterwards to become South Carolina and North Carolina, became a proprietary province in 1663. It was transferred back to the crown in 1729, when the patentees sold seven-eighths

1

1

of their lands and surrendered all of their powers of government. Prior to the date of its becoming a proprietary province there had been two attempts, though unsuccessful, to colonize this territory. In 1584, under a patent from Queen Elizabeth, Sir Walter Raleigh obtained the right to explore and settle any lands in North America not already occupied by any Christian prince, that is by any European power. Having such rights and privileges, Raleigh sent out during the next six years five different parties for exploration and settlement, but none of these were successful, at least for any appreciable duration. He spent practically forty thousand pounds, a large sum for those days, in these attempts. Realizing no returns and discouraged by his complete failure he surrendered his patent.[1] Again, in 1629, a second attempt was made toward colonizing this same territory. A patent was now issued by Charles I. to Sir Robert Heath, covering the lands from the thirty-first to the thirty-sixth degree north latitude; and the name of this grant was to be Carolina.[2] Heath made no settlement, assigning his rights and privileges, and the assignee likewise made none. This patent was declared null by the king in council, on the ground of no settlement having been made, as was required by the terms of the patent, and in 1663 Charles II. issued a charter for Carolina to eight lords proprietors, with the same territorial limits as specified in the grant to Heath; two years later these limits were enlarged, a new charter being issued which included all

[1] Hawks I, 11–17, 69–254.
[2] C. R. I, 5–13.

the lands between the degrees of twenty-nine and thirty-six and a half north latitude.[1] This territory was now no longer unsettled, as just prior to the issuing of the first charter the northern part of the grant was permanently settled by people from Virginia.[2]

These grantees were much more able to utilize their privileges and to discharge their duties than either of the other patentees had been. They were among the leading characters and statesmen of England, five of them holding high office of state, the most of them having been loyal to the crown during the tumultuous periods of the civil war and of the commonwealth. It is most probable that the king used this as a means of rewarding his able supporters, though in so doing he was giving away many of his powers and rights. These lords proprietors were: the Earl of Clarendon, the high chancellor; the Duke of Albemarle, the master of the horse and captain-general of all the forces; Lord, afterwards Earl, Craven; Lord Berkley, councillor; Lord Ashley, afterwards Earl of Shaftesbury, the chancellor of the exchequer; Sir George Carteret, councillor; Sir John Colleton; and Sir William Berkley, the governor of Virginia.

These patentees having all the powers of the Bishop of Durham, established in their province, or at least attempted to do so, a provincial system of government, after the type of the county-palatine of Durham; their "fundamental constitutions," which have become so famous, were based upon this idea—of a strong and

[1] C. R. I, 20–33, 102–114.
[2] Hening's Statutes at Large of Virginia I, 380–81.

highly centralized form of government.[1] That this
was their ideal there is much evidence; but in reality it
was impossible for such a system to be carried out, at
least to any very considerable extent, in a country as
new and thinly settled as Carolina was. In attempting
to establish such a system in their province they were
originating no new plan, as this was the old system of
feudal England and of many of the continental states.
By their charters they were made absolute lords over
Carolina, having all the powers of proprietors of the
soil and of the government which attended a possession
of the soil. In reality, however, their governing powers were subject to limitations; the circumstances
accompanying colonization in these lands operated very
strongly to change and even to set aside the political
theories and plans of such a nature. Unless specified
in the charters, the crown could place no restrictions
upon the patentees; their laws were in theory to be
binding upon the colonists. The king had no right to
disapprove them and, therefore, to set them aside, the
only body having the right to modify them being the
parliament of England.[2]

As we have stated, the northern portion of Carolina
had been settled to a slight degree prior to 1663; the
southern part was to be colonized under the proprietors. These two settlements were separated from each
other by a very considerable distance, the grant for
Carolina being large, and until 1691 each had its own
governor.[3] From this time to 1712 there was only one

[1] C. R. I, 22, 103, 187–206.

[2] C. R. II, 142–43.

[3] C. R. I, 48–50, 162–75, 181–82.

governor over the whole province; and he resided at
Charleston, in the southern settlement, while the northern one was under a deputy governor, appointed and
commissioned by him.[1] In fact, the proprietors now
intended to have but one governor and one legislative
assembly for their whole grant, though it had two separate and distinct settlements, and these a very considerable distance apart. But it was easily seen that the
two plantations were separated by too great a distance
for such a plan to operate at all successfully, and, therefore, the patentees granted to the colonists of the northern portion a separate legislative assembly, with a
deputy governor as their chief executive. By such an
arrangement this settlement, now known at times as
North Carolina, though usually called Albemarle, governed itself almost as its colonists desired, the deputy
governor having very little influence; he was not a
direct agent of the proprietors. This plan operating so
poorly for the proprietary interests, they, during the
latter part of 1710, determined upon having a separate
governor for North Carolina, as well as for South
Carolina, and Edward Hyde was at once appointed to
such an office, though his commission was not issued
until early in 1712.[2]

The period under the deputy governors was marked
by unsuccessful administration, in fact, by great disturbances, and in this respect was not unlike that of
the preceding seventeen years. For the first ten or
eleven years the proprietors exercised a fairly strong

[1] C. R. I, 373–82, 389–90, 554–57, 694–96, 707, 731, 773.
[2] C. R. I, 749–50, 841.

control over the colonists of the Albemarle province, but from 1674 to 1712 the colonists knew little governmental restraints excepting of their own making and drove out of office six of their fourteen governors or deputy governors.[1] During this time occurred two so-called rebellions. In 1677 came the Culpepper uprising, bringing great disturbance to the proprietors and to an extent to the colonists, closing their courts, subverting their government, and even casting into prison some of the deputies of the proprietors.[2] Its leader was John Culpepper, most likely a bold and ambitious man, and he was aided by some of the New England skippers. The colonists of North Carolina and the skippers of New England were unwilling to pay customs duties to the crown on the tobacco exported from the province, and avoid them they most certainly would, if possible. Their revolt was, therefore, purely on economic grounds. The insurrectionists armed themselves, seized the provincial and customs records, turned out of office Thomas Miller, a duly appointed collector of the king's customs, cleared and discharged ships without their paying duties on the tobacco with which they were laden, established courts, even for the hearing of cases involving life, and seized funds belonging to the treasury of England, collected as customs duties. They claimed that all this was done only for the time, until the duly appointed governor— Eastchurch—should arrive, and upon the ground that Miller was not the legal governor, not being appointed

[1] C. R. I, 48–220; Hawks II, 440–526.
[2] C. R. I, 256–61, 328; Hawks II, 464–81.

directly by the proprietors to such an office. Part of
this claim was well founded, as in fact Miller was not
the legal governor; he was only acting as president of
the council and *ex officio* chief executive until Eastchurch should come. His commission was issued by
Eastchurch, not by the proprietors. But he was duly
appointed by the crown as collector of customs and by
the proprietors as secretary of the province; and to
deprive him of the right to discharge the duties of these
offices, to cast him and several of the lawful magistrates
into prison, was wholly beyond law, and such conduct
will always be denounced as insurrection or rebellion.[1]

This insurrection, to be sure, was on the largest scale
of any of the disturbances which occurred prior to
1704, but it was by no means the only one, for during
this period the proprietors were not at all successful
in administering the affairs of their province. In fact
they were devoting very little intelligent attention
to either settlement, and especially to Albemarle. The
governors and deputy governors were weak and often
dishonest, while the colonists were simple farmers,
disposed to claim much for themselves in the way
of independent action.[2] From 1680 to 1704 their administration was of much better order, but this was to
be disturbed by another insurrection of considerable
proportions, covering practically the period from 1704
to 1710. The immediate cause of the beginning of this
trouble was the appointment of a deputy governor,
Robert Daniel, a man whose high church convictions

[1] C. R. I, 264–328; Hawks II, 468.
[2] C. R. I, 329–63, 373–84.

and ideas were very decided. When he came to North
Carolina, he attempted to carry out in this settlement
the plan which had been given to South Carolina, at
least for the time—that is to make it Anglican in its
church establishment. In some way he secured the
passage of an act to this effect. But the colonists had
many different religious convictions and probably a
goodly number cared very little for religious ideas at
all, certainly not if organized into a state establishment. The Quakers, though not numerous, held the
balance of power in several parts of the colony, and
they most certainly were opposed to an established
church.[1] This action on the part of Daniel, while not
being a new idea to the colonists, was still regarded by
the Dissenters as radical and contrary to their own
interests. Though it was evidently the original intention of the proprietors to have such an establishment
in the colony, still practically nothing was done for this
prior to 1700.[2] However, in 1701, the Anglicans had
sufficient influence to secure an act establishing a
church. By this a poll tax was to be levied upon all the
colonists for the support of the establishment. But
the opposition to such an act was very strong and
decided; it became so much so in the legislature of 1703
that the act would have been repealed had the proprietors not already disallowed it, not on the ground of
principle but of certain defects in its provisions.[3] The

[1] C. R. I, 521 et seq.; II, 867–82; Hawks II, 503–07; McCrady I,
367–69; Week's Relig. Dev., 33–4, 46 et seq.
[2] C. R. I, passim; Week's Relig. Dev., 32–36.
[3] C. R. I, 544, 559–61, 572, 601.

first struggle, therefore, for an established church
ended in failure and created a strong feeling among the
colonists, which assumed the spirit of rebellion; the so-
called Carey rebellion of 1705–1710 arose mainly from
religious causes. This spirit was strong when Daniel
came to the province.

In practice, at least, North Carolina had enjoyed
absolute toleration before 1701, in spite of the intentions of the proprietors.[1] Prior to this the Anglican
forces had been comparatively weak and the Dissenters
strong enough to prevent anything like an establishment. But now the forces in favor of an established
church were much strengthened by the formation of
the English society for the propagation of the gospel
and further by the appointment of Daniel as deputy
governor; they were now determined upon realizing
their desires and at once after Daniel's arrival they
obtained the passage of a vestry law, not so very different from the act of 1701. On the other hand, the
Dissenters were equally bent upon defeating this plan;
they struggled to have the law disallowed. They were
opposed to it on the ground of principle, desiring
complete religious toleration, as well as upon economic
grounds, because it meant the paying of taxes for its
support. North Carolina was not alone in this struggle, as her neighbor to the south was doing almost the
same thing and at almost the same time.[2]

---

[1] C. R. I, 34, 45, 54, 80, 81, 95, 100, 106, 109, 187–207; Week's Relig.
Dev., 13, 39.

[2] C. R. I, 709; II, 863–82; Week's Relig. Dev., 40–47; McCrady I,
402–50.

All of this was creating a spirit of unrest among the colonists, particularly concerning ecclesiastical questions. Consequently when the act of the British parliament, requiring the oath of allegiance from all English subjects to the queen and the heirs of the Protestant line,[1] arrived in North Carolina and was presented to the officers by the deputy governor, the Quakers at once refused to take the oath under the pretext that such action was inconsistent with their religious teachings. In consequence of this refusal, Daniel dismissed from office the Quakers who held positions in the lower house, council, or judicial system, and then secured the passage of an act declaring that no one could hold office without taking this oath of allegiance to the English crown.[2] Such a law would drive from office a goodly number of Dissenters, especially Quakers, who, though they had not been in public positions for any length of time, already held the balance of power. Daniel was removed from his position as chief executive, whether or not by the influence of the Quakers we do not know. Thomas Carey was appointed in 1705 to take his place.[4] Apparently Carey's appointment was very agreeable to the Quakers, but upon asking the officers to take the oath of allegiance to the queen he met with almost the same opposition that Daniel had. The Quakers were again dismissed from office and an act was passed placing a fine upon them for

1 Statutes of the Realm, 1 Anne c. 16.
2 C. R. I, 709.
3 C. R. I, 709; Hawks II, 440; McCrady I, 278–87, 720.
4 C. R. I, 709, 723, 725, 801; Week's Relig. Dev., 50–51.

holding office without taking the said oath.[1] His opponents in 1706 became so strongly opposed to him,
because of his official or personal conduct, that they
sent an agent to England whose specific mission was
to appeal to the proprietors against his administration, particularly against such requirements as he had
made in regard to the oath of allegiance; and most
probably this agent made an appeal against the establishment of the Anglican Church. His mission was in
part successful; at least Carey was removed from
office, though it is probable that his removal was due to
the fact that he had created a disturbance in enforcing the oath, and, therefore, meant in reality no yielding on the part of the patentees to the Dissenters.
That the proprietors were especially displeased with
Carey there is little evidence, his removal being mainly
a matter of compromise. He was perhaps very rigid
in his attempts to discharge certain official duties and
thereby offended the Dissenters who for a long period
had enjoyed complete toleration.[2] In fact the oath of
allegiance had nothing whatever to do with an Anglican
establishment or with taking away the toleration which
had hitherto been allowed, but in sentiment it was really
and closely connected with such ideas, at least in the
minds of the Dissenters. They thought that it was only
the beginning of a strong establishment, in fact, their
opposition to it was largely for this reason.

William Glover was now chosen president of the
council and as such became the chief executive. He,

[1] C. R. I, 709.
[2] C. R. I, 709, 779; Week's Relig. Dev., 51-55.

though regarded by many as a good man, personally
and professionally, met the same opposition as Daniel
and Carey had when he asked for the taking of the
oath of allegiance. The Dissenters in their reaction
against him went so far as to join Carey and follow
him as the leader of the opposition. Carey became the
actual governor of the Dissenters, now known as the
popular party, while Glover held the same office for the
Churchmen or conservatives. The province was, therefore, split asunder for the time, but toward the end of
1708 both factions were willing to refer their respective
claims to a general assembly which was then meeting,
or at least they made professions to this effect. In the
lower house of this assembly the Carey party had a
majority, and the two factions each had its council presided over by their leaders—Carey and Glover. The
lower house, being composed as it was, favored action
which was highly beneficial to the interests of the Dissenters and consequently passed an act which annulled
the taking of the oath of allegiance and also recognized
Carey as the governor. This action by the lower house
was at once concurred in by the council of the popular
faction. But Glover and his party, though they had
previously declared their intention of abiding by the
decision of the assembly, would not now acknowledge
such a proceeding as legal, claiming that he alone had
a commission from the proprietors to act as the chief
executive. A settlement of the points in dispute was
now no nearer than before, and great disorder consequently prevailed. The proprietors, perhaps thinking
to bring an end to this condition most satisfactorily by

recognizing the popular faction, at least for the time, declared in favor of Carey; and peace was restored after two years of confusion and disturbance.[1]

Evidently this plan of recognizing Carey as the chief executive was only temporary, as Edward Hyde arrived in 1710 as deputy governor, being appointed by the governor of South Carolina. But as the said governor died before a commission was issued to Hyde, there was some dispute for the time as to his assuming charge of affairs. However, having letters to the effect that he had been duly appointed, though not commissioned, he was accepted as president of the council. In 1712 he was appointed and commissioned by the proprietors as governor of North Carolina. This province was now separated from South Carolina and was given a distinct provincial government of its own.[2] The factional strife, when Hyde arrived as deputy governor, was not yet over; both parties were still at dagger's points with each other. Under him an assembly was held, early in 1711, in which the Anglicans had a clear majority. This was now the time for them to act in the way of revenge, and in a most vigorous and radical manner they acted. They made it sedition to speak against the government in any way whatever and not to take the oath of allegiance to the crown. They declared all suits and judgments of the period, July 24, 1708, to January 22, 1711, null and void. So great was their feeling against the Dissenters, who had been in power under Carey, that they proposed not only

[1] C. R. I, 696–99, 709–10, 763–72, 784–87; Week's Relig. Dev., 56–9.
[2] C. R. I, 731, 737, 775–79, 785, 841.

to have revenge but also to wipe out every vestige possible of the administration of the Dissenters. In addition to the sedition act, they arrested Carey and his chief followers, disfranchised the Quakers and made the Anglican church the establishment, the very thing against which the Dissenters had worked and struggled.[1] Such action on the part of the Churchmen enraged the popular party, as most naturally it would, and civil war was almost upon the colony, with Hyde and Carey as leaders of the opposing factions; it was prevented by the interference of the Virginia authorities in support of Hyde. This finally brought an end to the so-called Carey rebellion, July, 1711, after several years of confusion and chaos in the government.[2]

Though the Dissenters in this struggle finally lost, still by it they obtained a legal recognition in matters ecclesiastical. The act which had been passed concerning sedition and the keeping of the peace declared that not only the laws of the established church but also those allowing indulgence to Dissenters should be in force.[3] Now dissent, which had in a very indefinite way been allowed, was made legal, so that from this time to 1775 the province, while it had an established church, still allowed religious toleration in a perfectly legal manner. From this time to the end of the royal period there was some religious agitation but it was wholly upon constitutional lines.[4]

[1] C. R. I, 787–94; Week's Relig. Dev., 59–61.
[2] C. R. I, 758–63, 769, 774, 778, 780–95, 800–02, 831, 881, 912–22.
[3] C. R. I, 787–90.
[4] Week's Church and State, 9–11.

From the close of this disturbance to 1729 North
Carolina was free from such disorder as had occurred
at several times previously, and especially during the
periods 1677–1680, 1704–1711. What struggles there
were during the last eighteen years of the proprietary
government were constitutional and without violent or
radical action. The province was now under a separate governor directly appointed by the proprietors,
and the patentees gave much more attention to its
affairs than they had given for several years. The colonists also realized that they had gained rather little
by violence, as was manifested in the Culpepper and
Carey insurrections, and were now ready to act more
in accord with the principles of constitutional development, the proprietors being apparently willing to grant
to them a more liberal government. Both parties—
the patentees and the colonists—now directed their energies to preserve order, to collect the laws, and make
them known and obeyed. Prior to 1715 these were
very indefinite, not being collected or codified.[1] They
also, by an act of the assembly, regulated the qualifications of the electors and representatives, as well as the
method of holding the elections, declaring in favor of
biennial assemblies. The colonists now had control of
the making of the laws and were, therefore, no longer
under rigid regulations in this phase of their life.
They gave evidence of their substantial control over
legislation by passing laws, either wholly new ones or
old ones revised, which did not please the patentees,
as in their passage the proprietary interests were not

[1] C. R. I, 836 et seq.; II, passim.

well considered.[1] By the assemblies from 1716 to 1729 several other acts were passed, and were allowed by the proprietors, though they operated largely to the interests of the colonists, rather than to those of the proprietors.[2]

Thus far we have sketched, in meagre outline, the chief events of the proprietary period, having said little of the form of government which the patentees proposed to establish in their province or of the form of governmental machinery which was actually given to the colonists. It is now necessary, therefore, to take these under further consideration.

By their charters the patentees were given large powers in the administration of their extensive lands and in the government of those who should become settlers thereon. To them were granted the privilege and duty of enacting the laws, as well as enforcing them. They could at their discretion convert Carolina into a county-palatine, and govern it after the customs of the English counties-palatine, especially of the Durham type,[4] and it was most probably their intention sooner or later to establish a manorial form of government, particularly in its territorial system. But to do this required conditions different from those to be found in their wild and unsettled lands. It was necessary, therefore, to put in operation a more liberal and simple system, at least for the time, until the province

[1] C. R. II, 213–36; Swann, 2; MS. Laws.

[2] Swann, passim; MS. Laws.

[3] See Bassett's Const. Beginnings for much fuller treatment, also for a somewhat different point of view.

[4] C. R. I, 20–33, 103–14; II, 142–43.

should be more thickly settled. With such a plan in mind they issued certain proposals to the planters who would become permanent settlers. These were made in 1663 and again two years later, offering very liberal terms, especially democratic for the seventeenth century. By these certain concessions were made to the colonists, which remained practically permanent, at least so far as the colonists themselves were concerned, though the proprietors evidently meant them only as temporary—that is for the first settlers and for a time only for them. Not only were their concessions to the would-be settlers of the middle portion of their grant very liberal, but the instructions also which they sent out to the governors of the northern settlement were of the same spirit. Why the change from this liberal system to that of the "fundamental constitutions" of 1669–1670? These provided for a governmental machinery distinctly feudal and monarchical; the colonists were left with much smaller powers than they had under the first terms of settlement. To answer this question is by no means easy.

The first terms were offered in the "declarations and proposals," issued during the latter months of 1663. They were made for the most part to the people of the Barbadoes, who desired to form a colony in Carolina, on the Cape Fear River, but they were also offered to other English subjects who would become settlers in any part of the territory of the patentees. According to these terms the colonists were to have the right of nominating certain ones of their own number, one of whom the proprietors should appoint as governor and

2

six more as councillors; and these should administer
the affairs of the settlement. That these officers might
not become too arbitrary in their official conduct it was
provided that they should be nominated and chosen
every three years. The freeholders or their representatives were to have an important part in the legislation; they with the governor and councillors should
enact all the laws necessary for the proper administration of the settlement, provided the said acts were in
accord with the spirit of the laws of England. The
only other limitation upon the legislative powers of the
colonists was the necessity of their acts being approved
by the proprietors; when once thus approved, they were
to remain in force until repealed by the same body
which had passed them. The colonists also were to
have complete religious toleration and freedom, certainly a radically liberal concession for those times.[1]

No permanent settlement being made under these
terms, the proprietors regarded them as void. But
early in 1665 they signed another paper with the Barbadians, known as the "concessions and agreements";
and these were open to the Barbadians wherever they
might reside. They were again given very liberal privileges of establishing a plantation on the Cape Fear
River, but the same privileges were also offered to any
other settlement in Carolina. By these terms the patentees were to choose one of the colonists as the governor—a provision not quite so liberal as that of 1663
—and he in case of their failure to do so must select
either six or twelve councillors, a register and a sur-

[1] C. R. I, 43–46.

veyor-general, all being colonists. These officers, after
taking the oath of allegiance to the crown and of fidelity to the proprietors, were to administer the affairs
of the colonists, though in general accord with the instructions sent out by the patentees; and they with
twelve deputies chosen by the freemen and of the freemen constituted the legislative assembly, which made
the laws for the settlement. And to be a freeman was
very easy, the only requisite being the taking of the
same oaths as the officers were required to take. Complete freedom and toleration in religion were allowed,
conditioned only by the provision that no one in the
enjoyment of these could disturb the peace of the settlement. The assembly was to appoint an Anglican
minister, the Dissenters as churches were to choose their
own clergymen.[1]

Though the terms of 1665 were not as liberal as those
of two years earlier, still they were quite easy. It has
by some been doubted that the proprietors seriously
intended to carry out such liberal provisions, either
those of 1663 or 1665, but this doubt is not well founded.
That they fully meant to do so for a time is shown in
the commission which they issued in 1665 to Sir John
Yeamans as governor of the Barbadian settlement, and
also in the commission and instructions which they sent
out two years later to Samuel Stephens, governor of
Albemarle.[2] It is true that the form and spirit of
these terms were more liberal than was the custom of
the times and very much more so than those provided

[1] C. R. I, 79–92.
[2] C. R. I, 97–98, 162–75.

for in the "fundamental constitutions."[1]   These constitutions were the first attempt of the proprietors to
establish a manorial system, as provided for in the
charters; and evidently this had been their ideal, to be
realized sometime in the future. These were first
drawn up in 1669–1670, but no special effort was made
to put them into actual operation, at least for the time,
in the Albemarle settlement. Seeing that this province
was by no means sufficiently settled for such an elaborate machinery of government, the patentees continued to
allow many of their former concessions. The fact that
five different sets of these constitutions were drawn up,
the last one being in 1698, and that the later ones were
decided modifications of the first, would indicate that
the proprietors were experimenting as to what was in
practice best for North Carolina under its peculiar conditions.[2]

It seems that the first terms of settlement were leading to a spirit too greatly democratic and that the patentees, therefore, felt called on to check it,[3] and this
was to be done by the establishment of a manorial system, according to the constitutions of the great political
philosopher John Locke. As provided for in these
constitutions, Carolina was to be divided into counties,
and these into seigniories, baronies, precincts and colonies, with both lords and common freemen. The
lords were to possess two-fifths of the land; the colonists the remaining portion, upon grants from the lords;

[1] C. R. I, 187–205.
[2] C. R. II, 852–58; Hawks II, 184.
[3] C. R. I, 188; II, 852.

and the lords were to establish the old English manorial courts. Further, according to these constitutions, the proprietors were to organize an elaborate
system of administrative courts for regulating and controlling the provincial affairs in general, not in detail.
Within the province there should be a legislative assembly, elected biennially, which should make all the
laws for the colonists, subject to the confirmation of the
proprietors. In connection with this system was also
to be erected a church establishment, to be supported by
all of the colonists. But Dissenters might become settlers upon the condition of their paying high respect to
the whole government—the state and the church alike.
This plan, while having many of the old feudal ideas in
it, had also something of the new monarchical spirit.
But it was never seriously put into operation in North
Carolina; at most it was only a theoretical standard for
the proprietors, the colonists being governed by their
instructions, which at times had very little of the
manorial ideas in them.[1]

Whether these constitutions were to be fully carried
out or not, it is clear that the proprietors had now established, in theory at least, a very different system from
the one outlined in their early terms of settlement and
first instructions to the governors. The reason of the
change though not fully apparent, even after much consideration, is for the most part clear. Their first concessions were made chiefly to the Barbadians, who were
Englishmen and loyal to the English crown, having fled
from home during the stormy periods of the civil war

[1] C. R. I, 187–205; II, 852–58; Hawks II, 184.

and the commonwealth. The proprietors were for the most part loyal to the king and were consequently anxious to have such colonists, hence the liberal terms which they offered. A few of the Barbadians came and settled, though only for a short time, disbanding and leaving the province in 1667.[1] The reason why the same terms were granted to the first Albemarle settlers as to the Barbadians is not so apparent; possibly it was to induce people to become colonists in that section.[2] Perhaps these liberal privileges were changed to those of the "fundamental constitutions" because the Barbadians, to whom they were for the most part granted, had left the province, and also perhaps because of the fear of the democratic spirit, which was then manifesting itself among the colonists.

As has already been suggested, the government which the proprietors proposed for North Carolina was very different in many respects from that which they were actually able to put into operation. What the territorial, fiscal, judicial, and military systems were will be stated elsewhere. Here only the more formal aspects—the governor, the council, and the lower house of the legislature—will be discussed, and these only for the purpose of tracing the general development in these departments of government, with the view of making the transition from the proprietary to the royal province more clear.

The patentees did not organize as a body prior to 1669. Then they did something toward organization,

[1] C. R. I, 39–42, 46–47, 148–51, 157–59, 177–208.
[2] N. J. Archives, First series, I, 28 et seq.

forming the palatine's court—the court of the eldest proprietor—but this was the only one ever erected, out of several provided for in the "fundamental constitutions." Before this time Albemarle had been under a governor appointed in a rather loose kind of a manner, his powers and duties not being very specifically stated. But after the formation of the palatine's court he was much more exactly instructed and the provincial affairs were to be looked after according to a more definite plan. The governor was now to have and to exercise in the province the general powers of the palatine. However, he was not the only executive of the proprietors in the colony, as each patentee was supposed to have a deputy residing therein, and the governor must act with the concurrence of at least three of these.[1] By such a plan the chief executive in the province did not have much independent power. But still he was *ex officio* commander-in-chief of the army and militia, whenever there were any, vice admiral after 1697, when the province was placed under the direction of the admiralty court of England. He called and presided over the council, concurred in the acts of the general assembly, for the elections to which he issued writs, administered the oaths of fidelity and allegiance to the proprietors and the crown, and for the first thirty-seven years sat as president of the general court.[2] His appointment, commission and instructions issued directly from the proprietors until 1691, but for the next twenty-one years the chief officer of the province was only a deputy

[1] C. R. I, 179–83, 187–206.
[2] C. R. I, 181, 473.

governor, appointed and instructed by the governor of Carolina, residing in Charleston.[1]

In his general administrative duties the governor was aided much by the council. This body was made up for the first seven years of men appointed by the governor, but from 1670 to 1691 it was composed of ten members, five elected by the lower house as representing the colonists, and five deputies of the proprietors, while during the latter half of the proprietary period it was composed entirely of these deputies.[2] Throughout the whole period it had few powers apart from the governor. However, in conjunction with him it performed very considerable administrative work. The chief executive with its concurrence suspended for the time any officer, if deemed necessary, issued military commissions, reprieved criminals subject to appeal to the proprietors, made grants of land, and supplied all the offices established by the general assembly.[3] From 1670 to 1691 the governor and five deputies of the proprietors constituted the deputy palatine's court, and as such exercised powers over the ordinary council, this being composed largely of the proprietary deputies. So powerful did this court become that the regular council was abolished in 1691, and from this time to the end of the period the deputies with the governor exercised the chief administrative functions.[4]

There was a lower house of the legislature, representing the colonists, during practically the whole period

[1] C. R. I, 373–82, 389–90, 554–57, 694–96, 707–731, 733.

[2] C. R. II, 515 et seq.

[3] C. R. I, 79–92.

[4] C. R. I, 181–82, 193, 381, 384.

under the proprietors. This met with the council as one house until 1691, taking formal vote as one body; in actual practice, however, the governor and three deputies of the proprietors constituted a separate house. After this time the assembly met in two separate houses, and conducted all of the business upon the bicameral plan. This assembly, whether of one house or of two, enacted the laws, provided they were in accord with the laws of England and the desire of the proprietors, levied the taxes, established courts and provided for defence.[1]

It is evident from what has been stated in the foregoing pages that the proprietors were not very successful in their attempts at colonial administration in North Carolina. While the colonists at no time openly rebelled against the patentees, still quite frequently, as we have seen, they rebelled against their officers, especially their governors. During a part of the period this opposition took the shape of violence, but during the latter part it was only of the nature of constitutional complaint and struggle. The crown assumed the control of the province not because the colonists revolted against the patentees, but mainly because the crown had for some time seen that the proprietary provinces were fast drifting away from its regulation, and that they constituted an obstruction to a comprehensive colonial policy and system; and for this reason it was anxious to have the chance of regaining its control over them. The proprietors also were very willing to surrender all of their powers and burdens of government

[1] C. R. I, 79–101, 167, 381, 472, 629, 697, 780, 784–94.

and to sell most of their territory, as the South Carolina colonists had successfully revolted against them in 1719. During 1728 negotiations for such a transfer were entered upon and an agreement was reached, parliament confirming it during the next year. By this transfer all of the territory excepting one-eighth part became the lands of the crown, while all of the governmental powers reverted to the crown; North Carolina now became a royal province.[1] It was still a poor and small settlement, having a population of about 30,000 whites and 6,000 negroes,[2] and these lived within fifty miles of the sea-coast. With the transfer from proprietary to royal administration there was little change in the governmental machinery in its outward form. The governor, the council, and the lower house of the legislature continued, as did the administrative systems of land, finance, justice and defence. The chief difference was as to the immediate source of power; the crown now took the place of the proprietors.

This introduction having been made, we are ready to begin the study of the institutions under the crown.

[1] C. R. I, 721–23; III, 1, 12, 25–30, 37–47.
[2] C. R. III, 433.

CHAPTER II.

The Governor Under the Crown.

THE government of a royal province was in form much like that of the mother country. In all the provinces the crown was the chief executive and the ultimate source of governmental powers. It, however, delegated its authority in part to agents who resided among the colonists. Its executive power was bestowed upon an officer known as the governor. Each colony had such an officer, and his powers and duties were much the same in all of them. The governor was appointed by the crown, with an indefinite tenure of office, and was, therefore, responsible to the crown for all of his acts, and not to the people whose affairs he was to administer. Authority was conveyed to him through a commission, which was always a public document. At the appointment of this official, and from time to time thereafter, instructions were also issued by the crown for his guidance. They contained specific, though private, directions for him and the council, and the governor at times sent copies of certain clauses of these to the lower house. He was not legally bound to do this, but it was done occasionally in order to conciliate the representatives of the people.

These commissions and instructions served the colonists as charters, and the governor could not act, at least to any great extent, otherwise than according to them. He had some discretionary powers, but these were limited and temporary; for his acts of discretion he might be called into account by the crown officers in England.

A good many powers, with their corresponding duties, were bestowed upon the governor. By the advice and consent of the council, he was empowered to grant lands, according to the terms issued by the crown, or according to the terms of the acts of the legislature which the crown had approved; and these grants, when sealed with the seal of the province and recorded in the land office, were legal as against all persons, even against the king himself. The governor was ordered to exercise a careful oversight over the settlement of all lands thus granted. He could not allow larger grants than could be well settled and cultivated. He was forbidden to issue any grants whatever without a clause reserving the right to vacate them unless the quit-rents were paid and cultivation properly carried on. Over lands which escheated to the crown, or were forfeited, he was not given the power of final disposal until he had transmitted an account of them to the authorities in England and had received specific instructions from them.[1]

The governor, with the advice and consent of the council, appointed to all vacancies in the land office, and, in co-operation with the two houses of the legislature, enacted all the laws in regard to registration, alienation, transfer, title by occupation, validity of pat-

[1] C. R. III, 90–118, 496–98; V, 1103–44; VII, 137–42.

ents, resurvey, escheat, rent-rolls, and the number of acres to be granted to any one person.[1]   Quit-rents and the conditions of escheat and forfeiture neither he nor the legislature could determine, as these were reserved as the crown's exclusive right.   But he and the council decided whether lands had been settled according to the terms of the grants and whether they escheated or were forfeited.   Much of the work of the executive department was of this nature, hearing petitions for regrants of lands escheated or forfeited.[2]   It was also the duty of the governor to establish the court of exchequer and the court of claims, for the trial of cases arising from lands or their revenue.

In addition to these, the governor had many general administrative powers and duties.   He was the head of the whole administrative machinery of the province, and in this capacity watched all the parts of the system, and, so far as possible, directed its movements. His first duty, after arriving in the province, was to publish his commission and take all the oaths required by law and subscribe the test.   He must take the oaths of allegiance and supremacy to the king, of abjuration against the pretender, of office as governor of North Carolina, of office as governor of any royal province, and subscribe a declaration against the doctrine of transubstantiation.   These oaths show that he was to serve two different parties, the crown and the people of the province.   But as the crown, not the colonists, imposed the oaths upon him, he was legally bound to

[1] Law Revisals, passim.
[2] C. R. III–IX, passim.

serve the crown's interests, even at the expense of the people.[1]

He was required to administer these oaths and the test to all the members of the provincial council, and was given full power to suspend any councillor for sufficient cause. If the number of the council was less than seven, he was authorized to appoint to vacancies for the time, until the board of trade expressed its opinion; he could not fill vacancies if the membership was as large as seven. He was instructed to keep the board of trade supplied with a list of twelve persons fit for appointment as councillors. He could under no conditions increase the number of the council, nor could he suspend any councillor without a good and sufficient reason, and this must be done with the consent of a majority of this body. When he suspended any councillor he must send a full account of it to the board of trade and crown, which alone could render the final judgment in the matter. In case it became necessary for him to suspend a councillor, for reasons which he could not communicate to the council, he was given the power to do so, but he must at once transmit a full account of his action to the authorities at home.[2]

The governor was given the power and duty of keeping the seal of the province, of administering the oath in reference to his majesty's person to whomsoever he saw fit, of appointing certain officers and requiring them to take the oaths and test, of issuing out all moneys raised by acts of the assembly and expending the same

[1] C. R. III, 66–73.
[2] C. R. III, 90–118, 496–98; V, 1103–44.

for the support of the government, in accordance with the laws of the province, of appointing all fairs, marts, markets, ports and harbors, and of seeing that all the officers and ministers of the province were obedient to the chief executive.[1] Further, he was to investigate complaints and charges against former governors, and to look into the official conduct of all the officers, whenever it became necessary. He was given a careful oversight of the execution of the acts of trade and, in the absence of the surveyor-general of customs, he was directed to fill all vacancies, though temporarily, in his office.[2]

He was instructed to grant full liberty of conscience to all, excepting Papists, upon the condition that those enjoying the same gave no offence to good government; also to see that God was devoutly worshipped in the whole province, that the book of common prayer was read on every Sabbath and holiday, that the sacrament was administered according to the rites of the church of England, and that churches were kept up, ministers and parish work maintained. Nor could he permit any minister to take a benefice unless he had a certificate from the bishop of London. He was also ordered to allow the bishop of London much ecclesiastical control in many matters, though not in the collating to benefices, granting licenses of marriage and probating wills, these being reserved as the governor's exclusive right. Moreover, it was his duty to aid the bishop of London in all possible ways; to pass laws through the general

[1] C. R. III, 66–73.
[2] C. R. III, 103–09, 496–98; V, 1103–44; VII, 137–42.

assembly against blasphemy, profanity, adultery, for-
nication, incest, profaning the Lord's day, swearing
and drunkenness, and to recommend that the assembly
erect and support public schools; and to look after the
welfare of the Indians located within the province.[1]
It was likewise his duty to discourage and restrain any
attempts which might be made to establish manufac-
tures or trades in the province, which would in any
way be prejudicial to the kingdom of England—that
is competing industries.[2]   And lastly he was enjoined
to secure the passage of certain acts which would add
to the efficiency of the administrative system, and several were passed by the legislature for this purpose,
but frequently these were introduced and passed to
please the colonists rather than to increase the efficiency of the royal government.[3]

The governor was given these general powers, as well
as the specific ones, for no definite time; he always held
them at the pleasure of the crown.[4] In executing
them he was under many limitations. Burrington and
Johnston were directed to render full and accurate accounts of their acts of general administration to the
secretary of state and the board of trade. Dobbs and
his successors were instructed to correspond with the
secretary of state only when affairs demanded very
immediate attention from the crown, otherwise with the
board of trade;[5] this meant that the board of trade was

[1] C. R. III, 109–11.
[2] C. R. VI, 559.
[3] Law Revisals, passim.
[4] C. R. III, 66–73.
[5] C. R. V, 1103–44.

to have the larger part of the administration of colonial affairs and that the governor was to become their agent to a large extent. The commissions which he issued to the judges, justices of the peace and other officers, must have a clause stating that they were held during the pleasure of the crown. He was forbidden to fill any patent office, to which the crown had the right of appointment by warrant, except upon a vacancy or the suspension of any such officer by himself, and that for the time only. This provision placed a great limitation upon the governor's power of appointing to office, as the chief officials of the province were patent officers: the chief justice, secretary, attorney-general, provost-marshal, and the councillors.[1]

The governor had also all the powers that belonged to a captain-general or commander-in-chief: to levy, arm, muster, and command all persons residing in the province, to march or embark them for the purpose of resisting an enemy whenever occasion demanded it, and to transport the North Carolina militia and soldiers to any other American colony, if needed for its defence. He was given the power to execute martial law during the time of invasion, or at any other time when by the laws of England it might be executed; by the advice and consent of the council he was to build and supply forts, to appoint and commission captains, lieutenants, masters of ships, commanders and all the officers of martial law, according to 13 Charles II. He was directed to require the sheriffs to use all lawful means to keep the peace and to put down insurrections or

[1] C. R. III, 80, 107–08, 498.

3

riots, and he could lead the militia against those taking part in such actions.[1] The governor was also vice-admiral, and was given all the powers and duties of such an officer.[2]

In all matters of defence the governor's powers were less limited than in any other of his functions. This was very natural, as his province was subject to attacks by sea, by land from without, and by the Indians located within. Under these conditions it was necessary that the province have the best possible system of defence, and in order to accomplish this the crown delegated to the governor full military and naval powers. In civil affairs matters were not so pressing that they could not be considered by the board of trade and crown before a general decision was reached. In defence the governor and the council must have large powers and much discretion.

The governor was instructed to call a general assembly whenever occasion demanded it, and he and the council were to be the judges of the necessity. He was also instructed to make laws and ordinances for the welfare of the colonists and the benefit of the crown, provided that they were not repugnant to the laws of England. This always gave the final decision to the crown officers in England, and consequently made the governor only an agent in this particular. All the laws and ordinances passed by the assembly and assented to by himself must be sent to the crown within three months after their passing, for approval or dis-

[1] C. R. III, 66–73; VIII, 192–93.
[2] C. R. III, 212.

approval. The governor had a negative voice in the
passing of laws and ordinances by the assembly, and
none could be passed without his assent. He could
also prorogue or dissolve the assembly to prevent the
passing of certain bills, whenever he and the council
deemed it expedient.[1] But he could not determine the
manner of electing representatives, the number of members and how many should constitute a quorum, these
being defined in his instructions. It was his duty,
however, to see that the instructions on these points
were carried out. He was forbidden to assent to any
act of the legislature whereby its duration might be
limited or ascertained, its number increased or diminished, the qualifications of the electors or of the representatives fixed or altered, inconsistently with the
crown's rights. Neither could he assent to any act for
a gift from the assembly to himself, whereby it might
place him under its obligations.[2]

The governor alone could prorogue or dissolve the
assembly, though as a rule he consulted the council as
to when he should do this. In his power of assenting
to or rejecting bills he was limited by the require-
ment that he must send to the crown and board of
trade his reasons for so doing. Quite a number of the
acts assented to by him were disallowed by the crown.
This was done in the case of acts passed in 1739, 1740,
1754, 1756, 1765, 1768 and 1770.[3] He was under greater
restrictions and had less discretion in his law-making

[1] C. R. III, 66–73.
[2] C. R. V, 1103–44; VII, 137–42; VIII, 512–16.
[3] Law Revisals, passim.

powers than in any other of his functions. His land
grants and measures of defence, of general administration and justice, were not sent to the home government; he merely made reports concerning them. But
the acts of the legislature, to which he had given his
assent, were themselves examined by the crown officers
in England.

The governor also had judicial powers and duties.
He was instructed to erect and constitute such courts
of law and equity as he and the council deemed necessary for hearing and determining all cases, civil and
criminal, to have the oaths and test administered to all
persons connected with such courts, to appoint the
judges, excepting the chief justice whom the crown
appointed, commissioners of oyer and terminer, and
justices of the peace; also to pardon fines and forfeitures, when necessary, except in the case of treason
and wilful murder, in which he could only grant a
reprieve until the royal pleasure was known.[1]

In order to avoid long imprisonment, he was ordered
to appoint two courts of oyer and terminer to be held
yearly; also to see that all prisoners in case of treason
or felony had liberty to petition in open court for their
trials, to secure the passage of an act by which the
value of a man's estate requisite to entitle him to the
privilege of jury service should be determined, and to
see that no man's life, member, freehold or goods, was
taken or harmed otherwise than by the established laws.
He was directed to allow appeals from the courts of
justice to himself in the council, the court of chancery,

C. R. III, 66–73.

in civil causes where the value appealed for should exceed one hundred pounds sterling. He was also to allow appeals to the king in council in all cases of fines for misdemeanors in which the amount exceeded one hundred pounds sterling.[1]

There were, however, many limitations upon his judicial powers. He could not displace any judge or justice without a sufficient reason. The board of trade and crown alone could finally decide what constituted such a reason. He was not allowed to express any limitation of time in the commissions which he issued to judges or justices; they must always be for pleasure. Neither he nor his deputy could execute any of the offices of a judge or a justice. Nor could he abolish any court already erected without special leave from the crown, or allow any court of judicature to adjourn excepting upon good reasons. He was instructed to see that all persons committed to prison, except for treason and felony, had the immediate privilege of *habeas corpus,* and that no person set at large by an *habeas corpus* was recommitted for the same offence except by the court in which he was bound to appear.[2] And it was not within the power of the governor to assent to laws which appointed judges for good behavior, or to grant commissions to those thus appointed by acts of the legislature.[3]

Such were the constitutional powers and duties of the governor. In executing and discharging these he

[1] C. R. III, 90–118.
[2] C. R. III, 90–118.
[3] C. R. VII, 137–42.

had to look to the interest and welfare of two different parties—the crown and the colonists. He received his powers from the crown and was legally and directly responsible to it. He was intrusted with the administration of the affairs of the colonists, and was, therefore, indirectly responsible to them. By virtue of the fact that they bore the burdens of the government, paid the taxes, constituted the militia of the province and supplied its necessities, they exercised great influence over him. When he insisted upon acting to the full extent of his constitutional powers and exalted the royal rights and prerogatives, they stubbornly resisted him. When he yielded to any great extent to their assertion of rights and privileges independent of the crown, the home government censured him. The position of the governor was, therefore, not a pleasant one, especially when the colonists had been accustomed to act without much restraint, as was the case during the period of the proprietary government.

George Burrington, Esquire, was the first royal governor; it was his peculiar duty to show the colonists what a royal government in reality was. He was appointed and received his commission and instructions in 1730,[1] but did not begin to discharge his duties until February 25, 1731.[2] Sir Richard Everard, who was the last governor under the proprietors, was retained by the crown as acting chief executive until Burrington arrived.[3] Burrington had been one of the proprietary

[1] C. R. III, 65, 66, 74, 86, 87, 118–19.
[2] C. R. III, 211.
[3] C. R. II, 566; III, 2–74, passim.

governors, and as such had taken the oaths January 15, 1724.[1] As a governor under the proprietors he became much disliked, at least by many of the political leaders of the province. Chief Justice Gale, representing the opposition, went to England and made many serious charges against him. These charges, though supported by seven out of the ten councillors, were evidently much exaggerated and even false in several points, but they were sufficient to cause his removal, in July, 1725.[2] He and his opponents indulged in very severe language toward each other, rogue and villain being very common epithets, and after his displacement as a governor under the patentees many bills of indictment were brought against him for misconduct both as a citizen and as the chief executive. As he left the province soon after his removal, he never appeared to answer them. They were continued for several successive courts, but finally disappeared with an entry of *noli prosequi*. Though he had been very unpopular with the political leaders under the patentees, his appointment as the first royal governor was hailed with pleasure[3] by many of the colonists, who appear to have taken little part in preferring charges against him during his first administration. As proof of this the lower house of the first assembly which met under Everard sent an address to the proprietors, in which it declared that most of the charges of Gale and his friends were false and malicious, and that the province had pros-

[1] C. R. II, 515.
[2] C. R. II, 559–62, 566.
[3] C. R. II, 546, 647, 817; III, 134–35, 137–38.

pered and grown much under Burrington's care and industry.[1]

Burrington was an Englishman, of Devonshire.[2] The time of his birth is not known exactly, but from statements of his one would judge that he was born about 1685. He was, therefore, about forty-six years of age when he became the royal governor of North Carolina. He was a man of some education and of some good qualities. He, however, exalted the royal rights, ignored most of the political claims of the colonists, was violent in temper and speech, enjoyed a quarrel with his fellow officers, was a perfect master of abusive language, and was obstinate to a great degree, not being able to tolerate any difference of opinion. At the same time he was active and self-sacrificing in his attempts to promote the material interests of the province. As to his life before he became governor under the proprietors almost nothing is known. How he secured his appointment as royal governor, after he had been removed by the patentees because of many complaints of misconduct, is not known, but it seems that he had considerable influence with the Duke of Newcastle, secretary of state for the southern department.[3]

His welcome as the first royal governor did not last long. He soon became involved in conflicts and quarrels with the chief justice, attorney-general, judge of admiralty, secretary, council and lower house. Many

[1] C. R. II, 577-78.
[2] C. R. II, 480-81.
[3] C. R. III, passim.

of these officers were selfish, obstinate and uncompromising; they cared little for the royal administration and demanded of him rights and privileges which he could not legally grant. It soon became their custom to hinder him in practically all of his attempts to administer the affairs of the province. His administration was, therefore, one of great confusion and disorder. He and his opponents indulged in much personal abuse, and even went to the extent at times of making threats against each others' lives.[1]

His first legislature, that of 1731, during the first few days of the session, praised his ability, care and industry. But in a few weeks he was denouncing its members and calling them rascals and thieves. He had attempted to induce them to pass acts according to his instructions from the crown, but they insisted upon acting according to the laws passed by the legislature under the proprietors and during the period of 1729–1731, which acts the crown had not approved.[2] After several prorogations, he dissolved the assembly, without coming to an agreement and without passing any laws. He was then determined not to call another assembly for a considerable period, hoping that the members would change their position and yield to his requests. His second legislature did not meet until 1733. But there was no sign of a change on the part of the colonists or their representatives. The assembly at once declared that Burrington was oppressing the colonists, ignoring justice, using force, and governing in the most

[1] C. R. III, passim.
[2] C. R. III, 331–39.

arbitrary manner. Because of this declaration it was
dissolved. He called his third and last legislature in
1734, but was displaced by Johnston before he had time
to become involved in a quarrel with it.[1]

His relations with the councillors and other officers
were even less agreeable than those with the lower
house. Within three months after his arrival he was
in a bitter conflict with three councillors—Smith, Ashe
and Edmund Porter, and also with the secretary and
attorney-general. He was obstinate and intolerant
toward them, and they showed about the same disposition toward him. Neither side would make advances
toward a compromise, and the conflict went on. The
governor was left almost alone and his opponents used
every opportunity to hinder his administration. He
attempted to settle and govern the province according
to his commission and instructions, but most of the
other officers insisted upon constitutional rights independent of his instructions. When he began his administration there was really little government. The
general court had been set aside and some of the district courts discontinued, and the admiralty court had
been doing all kinds of business. He made several attempts to restore the province to a good government.[3]
By 1733 he seems to have accomplished something, at
least, in bringing the province to a condition of peace,
quiet and prosperity.[4] In the meantime Porter, Ashe

[1] C. R. III, 257–325, 536–611, 634–43.
[2] C. R. III, 139–41.
[3] C. R. III, 142–56.
[4] C. R. III, 429–37.

and Secretary Rice were sending reports to the board
of trade against his administration. They accused him
of usurping powers which did not belong to him. He
had suspended Porter from the council, and his instructions gave him, as he thought, power to do this. He
had created new precincts. They denied that he had
the power to do either. He had granted lands, as he
thought, according to the terms of his instructions.
They declared that he had no power to grant lands at
such high terms.[1] These gentlemen with the attorney-
general also accused him of using arbitrary powers in
regard to the council, courts of justice, land and other
matters.[2]

A great deal of bad feeling was shown by Burrington and his opponents. Who was the more to blame in
these conflicts it is difficult to say. Both parties went
to great extremes in their acts, and especially in their
denunciation of each other. The board of trade, in
writing to Burrington, in 1732, stated that he had perhaps nominated new councillors when there were as
many as seven, the number above which he could not
nominate, but that they were not able to come to an
absolutely certain conviction in the matter. They did
state that his conduct with the lower house had been
irregular and that his language to it had been intimidat-
ing. On the other hand the board of trade recognized
that both the lower house and the other officers had
claimed more rights than the governor could grant
them.[3]

[1] C. R. III, 325–31, 439–75.
[2] C. R. III, 356–82.
[3] C. R. III, 351–55.

His quarrels with his fellow officers show the weakest side of Burrington, and he was certainly not entirely responsible for them. In spite of these, he did much for the welfare of the province. His own statements, as well as those from his enemies, show that he made a close study of the material conditions of the province, that he understood the character and needs of the colonists to a considerable extent, and that he accomplished much for their welfare.[1] He looked carefully after the settlement of the lands and the making of internal improvements. He laid out roads, built bridges, sounded and explored several of the rivers. And for this, he states, he received only a vote of thanks from the assembly.[2] That the people appreciated his energy exercised for their welfare and that the province grew and prospered under him there are many proofs.[3] In his opening speeches to the assembly he asked it to act for the welfare of the whole province, to keep the bills of credit at par, to make the judicial system as efficient and convenient as possible, to appoint an agent who should reside in London and act for the province, to settle his salary, to provide an effectual way for direct trade with Europe and the West Indies, to support the church and clergy, and to pass acts requiring the proper registration of lands.[4] These requests show that he was working for the welfare of the colony as well as for that of the crown, and that he understood the

[1] C. R. III, 338 et seq.
[2] C. R. III, 29, 135, 287, 429–37, 577, 617.
[3] C. R. III, 194, 262; IV, 18–22.
[4] C. R. III, 257–58, 540–42, 636.

best needs of the colonists. In his speeches to the
legislatures of 1733 and 1734 he complained a good
deal about the fact that the former assemblies had accomplished nothing, and about their constitutional
claims which he could not grant. While his language
was not very diplomatic or politic, still for the most
part it was not unkind.

There were practically no complaints of his failure
to act, but many of his acting in an arbitrary way. He
sent long and frequent letters and reports to the authorities at home, as he was instructed to do. He
seems to have appointed to all the offices within his
power and to have looked carefully after the general
administration. While no laws were passed under him,
still this was not entirely his fault, as he held three
assemblies. He made no records of lands granted by
by him. That he issued warrants and patents for lands
is evident from what his opponents said about his
administration.[1] He did act in a very independent and
arbitrary way at times, but mainly according to his
interpretation of his powers and duties. The members
of the assembly and some of the councillors relied
upon the charters of 1663 and 1665 for their constitutional rights, and resisted most of his attempts to govern according to royal prerogative and rights. They
had long been accustomed to doing much as they
pleased in governmental affairs, and, therefore, demanded many rights and privileges for themselves
which he could not grant.[2] His great intolerance of

[1] Swann; C. R. III, 257–325, 457–75, 540–61, 634–43.
[2] C. R. III, 262, 265, 267, 270–72.

differences of opinion and violent conduct made for himself many strong enemies: Nathaniel Rice, John B. Ashe, Edmund Porter, John Montgomery, and other leaders in the colony, became and remained his opponents, and these were men whose influence he needed very much.[1] But even had he been very diplomatic, if at the same time he had insisted upon the royal rights, conflicts on fundamental and constitutional questions would have come. By a different personal conduct he might have avoided the personal struggles and quarrels, but it was almost inevitable that he and the legislature should become involved in grave conflicts. Their points of view on governmental questions were very different and would necessarily lead to disputes.

Burrington was promised out of the quit-rents a salary of seven hundred pounds yearly. The assembly did not and would not accept a plan for collecting these, and consequently he received very little toward his salary or expenses. He asked the crown for his expenses in making surveys and improvements, but his request was refused.[2]

Burrington's successor, Gabriel Johnston, Esquire, was appointed and commissioned in 1733, but did not assume control of provincial affairs until November, 1734. He remained in office until his death, July 17, 1752. He was by birth and education a Scotchman. His education, especially in the ancient languages, was good; he served for a time as professor of oriental lan-

[1] C. R. III, 377, 379, 385, 616, 617.
[2] C. R. III, 625, 626; preface, pp. x, xi.
[3] C. R. III, 438–39, 496–500, 642–43; IV, 1314.

guages in the University of St. Andrews. It is by
some authorities stated that he wrote several articles
on political and governmental questions, and that it
was due to these that he was appointed governor of
North Carolina, [1] whether this is true or not can not be
ascertained.

Most of the North Carolina historians have praised
his activity and character, but the records which he left
seem to indicate that he has been praised too highly.
He governed the province through a long period, and
under him it grew much in population and prosperity.
It is estimated that there were about 50,000 whites and
negroes in 1735 and about 90,000 in 1752. [2] An investigation into the causes of this increase in population
reveals the fact that Johnston had practically nothing
to do with it. He was evidently a man of many good
qualities; he was not profane as was Burrington,
neither was he drunken or violent in temper. He certainly did not know how to abuse his opponents as
did Burrington. As a man he therefore presents a
great contrast to his predecessor, but as a governor
he was in several respects less successful than Burrington, being careless in many important matters.

His administration was characterized by less conflict
than that of Burrington, there being practical agreement on many points between himself and the other
officers. When it began there was open hostility between the governor and practically all of the other
officers, but by the end of 1735 this had to a large

[1] C. R. IV, preface, p. iii.
[2] C. R. IV, preface, pp. vii, xx, xxi.

extent ceased. In 1734 little had been done toward putting in operation the royal government. Burrington had done something toward this, but not much; and what he had done was accomplished wholly by the executive, as he had never been able to influence the legislature to take any part in the new government. The collection of quit-rents due to the crown had not been provided for, and nothing had been done to improve the system of defence or militia.[1] Johnston had, therefore, many difficult tasks. Some of them he undertook with intelligence and energy; to others he paid little attention.

His opening speech to the assembly of 1735 shows that he was interested in the true welfare of the crown and of the colonists. He stated that he had called an early meeting of the legislature in order to put an end to the great confusion in the provincial affairs. He made no requests for himself, but only for good government. He asked the legislature to consider the question of quit-rents and currency, and to provide for the equitable collection of the one and to maintain the par value of the other. He further asked them to provide for the commercial welfare of the province and for the defence and militia.[2] The spirit of this speech and the manner in which he delivered it give sufficient evidence that he desired harmony and good feeling. He assured the assembly that it might examine all accounts of the expenditures of public moneys. In 1739 he again begged the representatives to lay aside all

[1] C. R. IV, 23–25, 242–43.
[2] C. R. IV, 77–79.

disputes and to act in harmony, urging them to provide
for better public worship; also for the collection of all
the provincial laws so that they might be better known
to the colonists, and for more efficient trade facilities.[1]
In 1744 he asked the assembly to assign more convenient places in which the courts should be held so that
they might become more efficient.[2] His conflicts with
the upper and lower houses of the legislature were
not very many or serious, and most important legislation was enacted during his administration. Between
1738 and 1750 seven laws concerning lands were
passed.[3] He was, to be sure, not the sole promoter
of these; some of them he requested, others were
passed by the legislature and merely assented to by
him. He secured the passage of three important militia acts, those of 1740, 1746 and 1749.[4] In all he held
nineteen sessions of the legislature and assented to one
hundred and thirty-one public acts, and only three of
these were repealed by the crown.[5] However, a study
of these acts and the part which he took in their passage
reveals the fact that he did not have very much to do
with them and that in many cases he gave considerable
privileges to the legislature, while assenting to its bills.
Several of these acts were intended more to secure the
interests of the colonists than the efficiency of the crown
government.

[1] C. R. IV, 356–57.
[2] C. R. IV, 720–21.
[3] Swann, 85, 90, 138, 155, 275, 285, 329.
[4] Swann, 119, 215, 305.
[5] Swann, 79–371, 85, 90, 116.

4

Johnston's relations with the council as an executive body were practically harmonious. He held many sessions of this body and considered a variety of subjects, but the chief business of the council under him was the hearing of petitions for grants of land and the issuing of warrants for such grants.[1]

He failed to keep the home authorities well informed as to colonial matters, especially during the last ten years of his administration. In his letters to the board of trade or secretary of state he never made any important statements concerning the growth of population, the prosperity of the colonists in farming, manufacturing or trade. In this he was far less active than Burrington or Dobbs. In 1745 the board of trade complained that it had been more than three years since they had received a letter from him, and they complained of not receiving any reports on provincial matters.[2] During the first six years of his administration he wrote many letters to the authorities in England, but after 1742 he was apparently very negligent in this. The board of trade did not receive a single letter or report from him between December, 1741, and June, 1746.[3] However, he wrote to them in 1747, and again in 1748, that he had been writing regularly, always sending duplicates.[4] In this he was either making a false statement or the facilities for carrying letters were far less efficient from 1741 to 1746 than at any

[1] C. R. IV, passim; MS. Warrants and Grants.
[2] C. R. IV, 756–57.
[3] C. R. IV, 797.
[4] C. R. IV, 797, 869.

other time during the royal government. It is probable, however, that the war which was then going on
did well nigh destroy the facilities for carrying mail.
In December, 1748, Corbin, Dobbs and others sent a
memorial to the Duke of Bedford, secretary of state
for the southern department, in which it was stated
that Johnston had long been very negligent in keeping
the home authorities informed concerning the province.
This memorial further charged that he had acted very
arbitrarily in judicial matters, that he had assented to
the issue of paper bills of credit when he had been specifically instructed not to do so, and that the government of the province was in great confusion.[1]   And at
about the same time the attorney-general, Thomas
Child, made like charges to the home government.[2]
However, James Abercromby, agent, during the early
part of the next year declared to the board of trade that
the above named complaints and charges had originated
in England, not in North Carolina, and that they were
false.[3]   There is some internal evidence in the two memorials of complaint against Johnston that Abercromby's statement was in part true.   In February, 1749,
the board of trade made a full report on the memorials.
This report stated that no letters had been received
between December, 1741, and June, 1746, and no journals of the legislature during this time excepting those
of the lower house for 1744, 1745, and 1746.   The report also stated that the evidence then available to the

[1] C. R. IV, 926.
[2] C. R. IV, 928.
[3] C. R. IV, 928–30.

board seemed to show that the memorialists against
Johnston were partially correct.[1] But Johnston in
writing to the board, September, 1751, declared that he
had sent the journals of the legislature regularly.[2]

It is difficult to judge what the truth is in regard to
this charge of negligence on the part of Johnston.
Shall we believe the reports of the board of trade or
the written statements of Johnston? The board has
stated that no letters or journals were received during
certain years, and Johnston has declared in writing
that he sent them. The records, as they now exist in
England, show that the board was correct in its statements. Still Johnston may be correct, as his letters
and reports might have miscarried; but this does not
appear to be very probable. It is most probable that
Johnston wrote few letters during his old age, and that
some of those which he did write miscarried. Though
he perhaps neglected to keep the home authorities well
and frequently informed during the last ten years of
his term, he did not fail to attend to his duties towards
the colonists; he held twelve sessions of the legislature after 1742 and passed several of the most important acts of his administration between 1742 and 1750.

He, like Burrington, received very little salary. In
1746, in writing to the board of trade, he stated that he
had received no pay during the past eight years.[3]
Even as late as 1791 there was still due to his family

[1] C. R. IV, 930–31, 935–36, 941.
[2] C. R. IV, 1075.
[3] C. R. IV, 792–93.

on his salary while governor over two thousand pounds.[1]

On the death of Johnston, Nathaniel Rice, the first councillor, became the acting governor. He died January 29, 1753. Matthew Rowan, the next councillor, then assumed control[2] and was the acting chief executive until Dobbs arrived. Rowan was very active and intelligent during his short administration. He sent to the home authorities good and pointed reports; and these were well received by the board of trade. He held several different meetings of the council for executive purposes, and one assembly which passed eight public acts.[3]

Johnston's successor, Arthur Dobbs, Esquire, was commissioned early in 1753, but did not reach the province until late in 1754. He took the oaths and test November 1, 1754, and remained in office until his death, March 28, 1765.[4] He was Scotch-Irish by birth. The exact date of his birth is not known, but it was probably before 1690. In 1720 he was high sheriff of Antrim county and later became a member of the Irish parliament. He was also engineer and surveyor-general of Ireland under Robert Walpole's administration as the prime minister of England. He was the author of books on the improvement and trade of his native country. It appears that his appointment as governor of North Carolina was largely due to his former ser-

[1] The New Annual Register, 1791, 128.
[2] C. R. IV, 1314; V, 17–18.
[3] C. R. V, 17, 18, 23–25, 29, 77, 108–09, 123–24; Davis, 1765, II, 17.
[4] C. R. V, 144g–144h; VI, 1320.

vices to the crown and to the fact that he had been an
officer of considerable ability and fine character.[1]
When he began his duties as governor he was at least
sixty-five years of age and knew nothing about the
colonists, their ideas and conditions. He was wholly
ignorant of the real resources of the province. Still he
was received with much pleasure, and at once began to
make himself acquainted with his new surroundings.
He had to govern at a critical time, when the English
were struggling with the French for the mastery of
North America, when the cause of Protestantism was
in conflict with Romanism, and when most of the Indians were in arms either against the English or French.
He entered into the conflict with much activity and zeal.
Under his leadership North Carolina did much for the
cause of the crown. He was a strong supporter of the
rights and privileges of the crown, even to the disadvantage of the colonists. Though a strong prerogative
governor, he showed much intelligence in his relation
with the province until about 1760, when poor health
began to impair his ability. From this time until 1765
he was more arbitrary and far less active. It was
during the last four years that the authorities in England made complaints about his obstinate policy and
his very poor reports.[2] On account of poor health he
made a request of the crown for a leave of absence for
one year. This leave was readily granted and Tryon
was commissioned as lieutenant-governor, April 26,
1764; his commission gave him the power of acting as

[1] C. R. V, preface, pp. iv–v.
[2] C. R. V, preface, pp. vi, vii, viii; VI, passim.

governor in the absence or upon the death of Dobbs.[1]
Tryon arrived in the province in October, but Dobbs
did not at once take his leave. He remained as the
actual chief executive until his death.[2]

Dobbs confessed his ignorance of the province and
at once after taking the oaths began to make an investigation into provincial affairs. He made a special examination of the defences of the colony, and of the
position and strength of the Indians located within or
on the borders. He also made full reports of the conditions, as far as he understood them, to the home
government. In 1755, 1756 and 1757, the board of
trade in writing to him expressed their great satisfac-
tion at his efforts to explore and defend the colony
against the Indians, and at the full reports which he
had sent to them. They also assured him that his
energy and zeal would receive the king's highest approval. In November, 1757, they expressed great
pleasure at his success in securing supplies from the
legislature with which to carry on the wars, to defend
North Carolina and to aid the other colonies.[3]

When his administration began the province was in
a good condition; there was much activity in agricul-
tural pursuits and much general prosperity. There
were about 100,000 people in the province in 1754, and
though his term was one of almost constant war, still
by 1765 the population had increased to about 125,000.[4]

[1] C. R. VI, 1043–44.
[2] C. R. VI, 1320.
[3] C. R. V, 413–17, 419–20, 563, 748, 786.
[4] C. R. V, preface, pp. xxx–ix.

He showed much interest in informing the home authorities concerning the material conditions of the province, especially during the first five years of his administration. He and the council issued a good many land warrants and grants, though some of them were not judiciously given.[1]

His relations with the lower house of the legislature were cordial until about 1760, and after this there were no very serious quarrels between them. The representatives granted his requests for money without very much discussion until 1760; from 1760 to 1762 they frequently complained of his demands for money and of his whole administration. These complaints were made chiefly because he often asked for money with which to carry on the war against the French and Indians. In all he held seventeen assemblies and passed one hundred and fifty-five public acts, only five of which were disallowed by the crown. He enacted two good militia laws, only slightly changing the acts of 1746 and 1749. He secured the passage of five fairly good laws concerning land.[2] At almost every session of the legislature from 1754 to 1762 he asked for troops, supplies, fortifications, stores and magazines;[3] the defence of the province and aid to the crown were his chief aims. He insisted on these, even to the neglect of everything else. It was necessary to provide for the defence of the colony, and the legislature agreed

[1] MS. Warrants and Grants; C. R. V–VI, passim.

[2] Davis, 1765, II, 34–386, 35, 70–72, 82–84, 192–97, 211–12, 309–15, 331–32.

[3] C. R. V, 233–36, 496, 639, 831; VI, 133, 802.

with him in this. But to Dobbs it was much more important to aid the other colonies, especially those in the north than to defend or work for the interests solely of North Carolina. To drive the French from North America seemed to him of far more importance than to make North Carolina a very prosperous province. The legislators on the other hand cared much more for their own province and its welfare than they did about the French. To them the defence of the province was the chief object. It was due to these different points of view that Dobbs and the assembly could not agree on several important questions, especially from 1760 to 1762. Though he gave his greatest energy and zeal to making war, he still asked the legislature to provide a permanent and suitable fund for the governor and government, a better system of teaching religion to the colonists, a more careful collection of the taxes and quit-rents, and a more just financial system.[1] In May, 1760, the lower house drew up fourteen resolutions of complaint against his administration.[2] But he, in a letter to the board of trade during August of the same year, defended himself against these charges. One of them was that he had not judiciously applied the funds granted by the assembly as aids to the crown. He denied this, and as the evidence goes to show, he was justified in so doing. To its charge, that he had received one thousand pounds out of the dividend from England to the American colonies and that he had not accounted for the same, he answered that he had been compelled

[1] C. R. V, 233–36, 496–97, 659–60.
[2] C. R. VI, 410–13.

to use this for the troops, as the lower house had not
made sufficient provision for them. The other complaints were of a more general nature. The records
which both parties left indicate that Dobbs was to a
large extent discharging his duty according to his instructions. He was very uncompromising in this at
times, but there is no doubt of his sincerity and honesty. While he was making too many claims in favor
of prerogative government, the lower house was at the
same time claiming rights and privileges which did
not constitutionally belong to it.

In some of the extreme positions the board of trade
did not sustain him. In April, 1761, they, in a letter to
him, declared that he had hindered his majesty's service
by insisting too much on trivial points and on the mere
letter of his instructions, that he had not considered
sufficiently the difficulties of the situation, and consequently had brought on a dispute with the legislature
at a time which demanded harmony above all things.
He had claimed the right of nominating an agent to
represent the province in England. The lower house
also had claimed this as its exclusive right. No agreement could be reached on this, and Dobbs rejected a
supply bill because it contained an agent clause, at a
time when the crown's service demanded the money.
The board declared that he had no right to insist
on the nomination of the agent, that the lower house had
the right to nominate such an officer. They further
stated that his rejection of an aid bill because of a failure to agree on one point was trivial and foolish.[1]

[1] C. R. VI, 538–41.

From this time until the end of his administration the home authorities did not sustain him in several of his acts. During December, 1761, the board of trade in a report to the crown, concerning three acts passed by the legislature and agreed to by Dobbs in May, 1760, relating to superior courts, inferior courts and orphans, advised it to disallow them because of the extraordinary clauses concerning the qualifications of associate judges, the duration of their commissions, and the jurisdiction of the inferior courts. They also reprimanded Dobbs for assenting to such acts, because they were in direct violation of his instructions. The board of trade again in 1762 informed the king that Dobbs in assenting to the vestry and clergy act of 1760 had shown another evidence of inattention to his instructions.[1] It should be stated, however, that in these acts Dobbs had been under much compulsion from the lower house. He had to assent to some of them in order to secure the passage of any acts at all. But in spite of such statements from the board of trade there is evidence that they and the other officers in England had much respect for Dobbs, though he was now in old age and poor health. Before 1761 they had full sympathy and appreciation for his services, and they continued to respect him to the end. As evidence of this, Lord Egremont, secretary of state for the southern department, November, 1762, in a letter to him declared that the king was especially sensible of his great zeal in raising troops for the war.[2]

[1] C. R. VI, 589–91, 723.
[2] C. R. VI, 736.

Concerning his salary he had practically the same experiences as the former governors. In March, 1764, he wrote to the board of trade that the lower house had refused to settle a salary on him and to pay the rent of a house for his use.[1] Though no provision was made for a definite support for him, both houses had much respect for his administration, even to the end. In November, 1764, they made him addresses, in which they declared that he had been wise, steady and uniform in working for his majesty and the province, and that his administration had been good and pure.[2]

Upon the death of Dobbs, William Tryon, who had already arrived with a commission as lieutenant-governor, became the chief executive. He was given a commission as governor July 19, 1765, and took the oaths and test on December 20 of the same year.[3] He remained as the governor until June 30, 1771,[4] when he resigned to become the chief executive of the colony of New York. Tryon was an Englishman by birth and a soldier by profession. He had gone through the ranks to lieutenant-colonelcy, and after he left North Carolina won the titles of colonel, major and major-general. He was a man of much influence at the court. For this reason, as well as for his ability, he secured the appointment as governor of North Carolina.[5] In his relations with the colonists he was shrewd and diplo-

[1] C. R. VI, 1039–41.
[2] C. R. VI, 1249, 1316.
[3] C. R. VII, 4, 133.
[4] C. R. VIII, 627.
[5] C. R. VIII, preface, pp. xxxiv–xxxviii.

matic, proud and fond of the show of a soldier's life. He was still young when he came to the province and showed much activity and ability in keeping himself in high favor with its leaders.

In 1767 he wrote to the secretary of state for the southern department a long report on the polity of the province. In this he stated with much clearness how the province was governed, what officers, executive, legislative, judicial, there were, how these performed their duties and what rights and privileges they had.[1] From the standpoint of style and comprehensiveness this is more than an ordinary document. It gives evidence that Tryon, though a soldier by profession, knew much of government and politics and that his ability was considerable. It is not strange, therefore, that the king was highly pleased with such a paper and with his administration up to the time of the writing of it.[2]

It was during his administration that the insurrection known as the war of the "regulation" occurred. This was an uprising among the people of the counties of the western part of the province, Orange being the center. These people complained of many and grievous burdens of government, that they were unjustly taxed, and that they were refused justice at the hands of the provincial officers. Tryon was ready to act in keeping the peace of the whole province and in putting down this insurrection. In April, 1768, he issued a proclamation to the colonel of the militia of Orange County, ordering him to be ready to act against the

[1] C. R. VII, 472–91.
[2] C. R. VII, 737–38.

"regulators" in case of need. On the same day he by another proclamation commanded the insurrectionists to disperse and go to their homes, and gave orders to all officers and citizens to put down the insurrection, if the "regulators" should go to extremes.[1] He made a military expedition to Hillsborough, the official town of Orange County, in September of this year, with a view of settling these troubles,[2] and again during the early part of 1771. The second expedition completely crushed the insurrection of about two thousand men.[3] He put down the "regulators" by force of arms, but did little or nothing to remedy the causes which brought on the uprising.

He issued several grants of land and assented to three acts concerning the administration of the lands.[5] In his ideas concerning the militia and defence he was not original, as he carried out substantially the same policy as Johnston and Dobbs. He held six assemblies and passed one hundred and sixteen public acts.[6] Of these the crown disallowed eight, more than it disallowed of those passed by Johnston or Dobbs. And a study of the legislative acts of Tryon's administration reveals the fact that he did not attempt very seriously to improve the conditions of the colony, his chief energies being given toward keeping himself in high favor with the political leaders.

[1] C. R. VII, 718–19, 721.
[2] C. R. VII, 887–88.
[3] C. R. VIII, 574–621.
[4] MS. Warrants and Grants.
[5] Davis, 1773, 344, 464, 491.
[6] Davis, 1765, II, 393; Davis, 1773, 338–495.

In his dealings with the members of the lower house, as with the other officers, he was very diplomatic and clever, and consequently left no record of serious conflict with any of them. In his opening speeches to the assembly he showed much ability in managing men; he made them understand his wants and requests, but never made opponents of them by the manner in which he spoke. He asked for the continuance of the fortifications at Fort Johnston and for an efficient provision for powder and lead. He asked them to continue the judicial system of Dobbs, to look after the condition of the public finances and to make a better provision for the sheriffs. He urged them to consider the importance of the office of sheriff, to see that more fees were allowed and that better men were appointed to the office. In 1768 he laid before the assembly a full account of the "regulation" troubles in the western counties, and asked it to make a careful investigation into the matter, to find out what the causes were, to relieve the insurgents if they suffered real grievances, and especially to provide a military force with which to put them down. In this recommendation he gave evidence that he was much more anxious for a suitable armed force, with which to crush the insurrection, than he was for the correction of the abuses. And in 1770 he made the statement to the assembly that he would be glad to see a public school established in the western counties, for the purpose of teaching and educating the men of the frontier.[1]

He thought that a strong military force would have

[1] C. R. VII, 292–95, 890–92; VIII, 283–85.

a good influence upon the colonists, especially those in the west. To him the highest product of good government was a well organized and equipped army. When, in 1767, he surveyed the boundary line for the Cherokee Indians he took along with the surveyors a considerable cavalcade of soldiers. This was done in a time of peace, when there was no longer any fear of the Cherokees, and at a cost to the colonists of about 1490 pounds.[1]   Still there was some need of convincing the Indians of the power of the royal government. He was very extravagant in his ideas and consequently was always in need of much money, either for himself or his government. While his predecessors had received very little of their salary, he by clever diplomacy obtained about all the money he desired. His military expeditions to the western counties in 1768 and 1771 cost about 44,844 pounds.[2]   He was also able to persuade the assembly to build for him a palace at a cost of 15,000 pounds.[3]

Though he had performed no service for the province of a permanent nature—excepting his successful defeat of the "regulators," which, while it put down an insurrection of about two thousand poor people and thereby exalted the power of the crown, increased the debt of the colony by almost 50,000 pounds[4]—his departure was much lamented by many of the political leaders. In December, 1770, both houses of the legisla-

[1] C. R. VII, 991–1009.
[2] C. R. VII, 887–88; VIII, 574–623.
[3] Davis, 1773, 342–43, 394–95.
[4] Unless otherwise stated, in proclamation.

made addresses to him, in which they stated that he had done all in his power to aid the province. In July, 1771, President Hassell in writing to Secretary Hillsborough declared that no governor had left the province more beloved by the people.[1] However, these complimentary statements from the legislature and the acting chief executive can not be taken with too much seriousness. There is much evidence to show that Tryon made himself very agreeable to many of the colonists, especially the political leaders and influential men, and that he commanded their support and affection to a high degree. But his success in winning the confidence of the officers of the government in England and in the province was due to a very considerable extent to his tact rather than to what he really accomplished. He was successful as a soldier, but in solving the great problems of his administration he accomplished little.

When Tryon left, James Hassell, the first councillor, became the acting governor, and as such took the oaths, July 1, 1771.[2] In December, 1770, Josiah Martin, Esquire, was commissioned as Tryon's successor. He did not assume control of the administration until August 12, 1771.[3] He remained in office until the royal government was overthrown by the revolution; and on August 8, 1775, from his majesty's sloop Cruizer he issued his last proclamation.[4]

[1] C. R. VIII, 289–90, 311–12; IX, 9.
[2] C. R. IX, 3–4.
[3] C. R. VIII, 267, 512–16; IX, 15.
[4] C. R. X, 141–51.

5

Martin was an Englishman, and was about thirty-five years of age when he began his duties as governor. He was a soldier in the British army from 1756 to 1769, when he sold his commission. As a soldier he had served as ensign and major, and had won the rank of lieutenant-colonel.[1] As a governor he was plain, blunt, lacking in tact, and was inclined to exalt prerogative too highly. He never could understand the sentiments and demands of the colonists; he could not see or appreciate their point of view, and was much like Burrington in being intolerant of differences of opinion. To him it was absolutely necessary to carry out, even to the letter, his instructions from the crown. Tryon had been an excellent servant of the crown, and he also knew how to make himself agreeable to many people. In this latter quality Martin was wholly lacking; he could not make himself agreeable to many of the colonists. The difficulties of his situation, his lack of tact, his exaltation of the royal prerogative at a time when the colonists were claiming many rights of self-government—all caused him much trouble. He began his administration with many difficult problems and tasks. He had to pacify the "regulators" whom Tryon had put down by force of arms. He had to face large debts and a poor judicial system; both of which involved problems which Tryon had not solved.

He held three assemblies and passed eighty-nine public acts. The fact that none of these was disallowed by the crown[2] is evidence that he was much re-

[1] C. R. IX, preface, pp. iii–iv.
[2] Davis, 1773, 496–566; Iredell, 1791, 270–74.

spected by the crown officers in England. In his opening speeches to the assembly he recommended several
things which were for the true interest of the province.
He asked it to provide a good system of militia and
defence, to investigate the causes which led to the
"regulation" war, to remove the abuses, to pardon
those guilty of insurrection, and to enact laws for the
more efficient administration of finance and justice.[1]
He made no demands for himself, as Tryon was in the
habit of doing, but only for the crown's interest in the
colony. Though his requests were wholly unselfish
and really for the welfare of the province, he and the
legislature became involved in many and serious conflicts, especially over fiscal and judicial questions.
The legislature insisted upon claims which his instructions compelled him to reject, and he was obstinate in
commanding them to agree to the very letter of his
instructions. In spite of the fact that eighty-nine public acts were passed and agreed to by him, all the legislative sessions under him were stormy, especially so
whenever judicial or fiscal questions came up.

In his struggle with the legislature the home authorities in the main stood by him. The board of trade and
crown approved of his zeal and interest.[2] Expres-
sions of this approval came at many different times.
Lord Dartmouth, secretary of the American department, in writing to him, May 4, 1774, lamented the very
bad state of affairs in the province but declared that
he and the other authorities highly approved of Mar-

[1] C. R. IX, 101–03, 397, 833.
[2] C. R. IX, 277, 618.

tin's acts, especially during the stormy session of the
assembly, March, 1774, when he had adjourned it after
he saw no hope of success for the royal cause. Again
in October of the same year Dartmouth declared to him
that the king regarded him as a most faithful servant.
In this letter, Dartmouth expressed the opinion of the
crown in regard to the extreme ideas and demands of
the assembly, that they were making unwarrantable
encroachments.[1]

After the session of March, 1774, Martin felt that
everything was in a very serious condition in the
American colonies, and that the people of North Carolina were too much excited over the struggles of the
last assembly to call another for the time. The colonists were not to be kept quiet by this means. John
Harvey called a provincial congress for August 25,
1774, and the freeholders, at least the more radical
ones, elected deputies to it.[2] This was done without
the consent of the governor, and he by a proclamation
complained of such revolutionary proceeding.[3] Still
the congress met at Newbern at the appointed time.
It elected and instructed three delegates to the proposed continental congress at Philadelphia and adopted
a large number of resolutions, defining their position
against the bad government of the crown's ministers.[4]
It then adjourned, August 27. The first continental
congress asked for a second at Philadelphia in 1775.

[1] C. R. IX, 988, 1077.
[2] C. R. IX, 1031–41.
[3] C. R. IX, 1029–30.
[4] C. R. IX, 1041–49.

In February, 1775, John Harvey called for a second provincial congress, to meet April 3.[1] Martin issued a proclamation against this.[2] The election, however, took place and the congress met at Newbern at the designated time, in spite of his proclamation.[3] It highly approved of the actions of the first continental congress and chose delegates to the second. This provincial congress met at the same time and place as the assembly which Martin had called. Most of the members of the lower house were also in the congress. The governor could, therefore, do nothing with the assembly and dissolved it on April 8.[4]

Martin now did not feel safe at Newbern, and in May, 1775, went to Fort Johnston, at the mouth of the Cape Fear River. From this time he was not the actual governor, and there was no longer a royal government in the province.[5] He saw so much of rebellion and revolution all over the colony that he did not feel safe at Fort Johnston and went on board His Majesty's sloop Cruizer.[6] From the sloop he issued several proclamations, but these were wholly unheeded by the colonists.[7]

Upon the whole, therefore, the royal governors of North Carolina make a good showing, though they were the agents of an inefficient system. The machinery of English colonial government in the eighteenth century

[1] C. R. IX, 1145.
[2] C. R. IX, 1145–46.
[3] C. R. IX, 1178–85.
[4] C. R. IX, 1178–79, 1187–1205.
[5] C. R. IX, 1254–58.
[6] C. R. X, 1–69.
[7] C. R. X, 141–51.

lacked much in unity and dispatch. The board of trade was slow in making its decision on colonial matters, and the law officers of the crown required still more time. The secretaries and the king did not pay very great attention to many matters, though important. The records of North Carolina afford much evidence of the carelessness and dilatory habits of the home government. With the exception of the last ten years of Johnston's administration, the governors were careful to keep the crown well informed respecting provincial affairs. During the whole period they attended to the administration of the province with much interest, though at times with little intelligence. They all seemed to have as their chief aim the welfare of the crown and of the province. The records show that they were honest servants; their mistakes were mainly those of judgment. At times they adhered obstinately to the letter of their instructions and in so doing rendered their position and that of the crown weak. They often forgot that the people under the proprietors governed themselves almost without restraint, and often ignored the fact that a people with such a history would not readily yield to prerogative government. So far as actual achievements are concerned, Burrington and Martin did the least. But it must be remembered that Burrington was the first royal governor and that consequently he had to make the first attempts to uphold the royal prerogative, an institution the spirit of which they did not understand or appreciate. Martin was the last governor, and as such had to face the revolutionary spirit then abroad in all the American colonies.

CHAPTER III.

The Council Under the Crown.

The position of the governor in a royal province has been discussed. He was the chief executive, but by no means the whole of the executive department. In exercising his powers and discharging his duties it was necessary for him to consult the council, and in several matters he could not act without their advice and consent. He was not only restricted by the fact that he must make reports of his acts to the board of trade and crown, but he must also act according to the advice of his councillors. As a rule the governor's relations with the council were close and friendly; they both represented the same institution, the crown, and were amenable for their acts to the same power. Burrington's relations with the council, however, were very unpleasant, chiefly for personal reasons, and Martin during the last few months of his administration could not act in harmony with this body, chiefly because the councillors were taking the side of the colonists in their extreme demands, while he was exalting prerogative government.

The council was provided for in the commissions and instructions from the crown to the governor; the first list of councillors was as a rule named in the instructions to the governor. When a vacancy occurred

71

in this, the king, with the co-operation of the board of trade, filled it by giving a commission to the one they approved out of the number recommended by the governor. The commissions and instructions to the governor also specified the powers and privileges of the council. The councillors, therefore, did not receive their powers from the people of the province and hence were not so much inclined to enter into their feelings. They were largely under the control of the governor. He might suspend any of them for misconduct or failure to discharge their duties, but the reasons for so doing must always be sent to the board of trade and king, who had a final decision in the matter. This provision placed them, as well as the governor, under the ultimate control of the authorities in England. Burrington's instructions stated that, if any councillor residing in the province should wilfully absent himself from the council when duly summoned, and without lawful cause should persist therein after being admonished, the governor might suspend him until the crown's pleasure was known.[1] The instructions to the later governors contained substantially the same provisions. Several suspensions were made by the governor, but some of those suspended by him were restored by the crown. The governor could also fill vacancies, if the number of councillors fell below seven, but this was done subject to the royal will.

The council acted as an adjunct to the governor and was, therefore, in this respect an executive body. When the governor died or was absent from the prov-

[1] C. R. III, 93.

ince, the president of the council acted as the chief executive for the time, as was the case of presidents Rice, Rowan and Hassell. The same body also constituted the upper house of the legislature. As the upper house the council held its sessions at the same time with the lower house. Sometimes it was in session as a semi-legislative body when the lower house was not in session, and as such it and the governor passed certain necessary ordinances.

The council as an executive body had a very considerable share in the administration of the territorial system and administration. The governor was ordered to exercise his territorial powers by their advice and consent;[1] and in this he rarely disobeyed his instructions. They, with the chief executive, issued the warrants and grants,[2] decided upon the question whether lands should be granted to certain persons and whether lands were escheated or forfeited. It was their duty also to see that the quit-rents were properly collected. They heard many complaints about the legality of grants, decided whether quit-rents were payable in certain products, and what should be the value of such products, summoned persons before them to show why they held or laid claim to lands, heard petitions for regrants, erected a court of exchequer for adjusting all cases relating to the crown's revenue from lands, and appointed assistant barons to the said court. They also ordered that the governor sit in the council at certain times to hear and deter-

[1] C. R. III, 101.
[2] MS. Warrants and Grants.

mine all claims pertaining to land, and decided upon the time when the surveyor-general should make his returns.[1]

The council also shared largely in the general administration of the province. In this the governor could not act without the advice and consent of at least five councillors, unless upon very urgent business, when he might advise with only three.[2] In this capacity as a general administrative body the council had a large variety of duties. They ordered letters patent to be issued to the chief justice, secretary and other patent officers whom the crown had appointed, which instructed them to begin their duties in the province, and ordered commissions of the peace to be issued appointing certain persons justices of the peace. They appointed administrators of certain private estates and sat in judgment over the administration,[3] heard complaints against the officers of the province and at times advised the governor to suspend them from their office, even that of the council, recommended to the governor persons fit to fill the vacancies pending the royal pleasure, heard and granted petitions for new precincts, summoned precinct treasurers to appear before them and exhibit their accounts, ordered sheriffs to complete the collection of taxes by certain times, considered all questions pertaining to the affairs of the Indians located within or on the borders of the prov-

[1] C. R. III, 219, 276, 401, 424–26; IV, 36–38, 40, 43, 44, 53, 71; V, 489, 656; VI, 1073–76; VIII, 160–64, 192; MS. Warrants and Grants.

[2] C. R. III, 91.

[3] C. R. III, 214–15, 217, 224, 234.

ince, heard and advised the governor to grant petitions for reprieve to certain persons under heavy sentences, and finally could appoint a committee to act jointly with a committee from the lower house in examining and auditing all public claims and accounts.[1] While in many of these matters the council merely advised, still the governor rarely acted contrary to their advice. Very frequently matters were left entirely to a majority of the councillors and the governor acted in strict accordance with their decision.

The council had some judicial powers and duties, though these were mainly of the nature of advice. They advised that commissions be issued appointing assistant justices of the general court, and that courts of oyer and terminer be held at certain times and places. They, with the governor, issued commissions of the peace, appointing themselves, the secretary, attorney-general, assistant justices and the chairmen of the precincts—all justices of the peace. The governor in the council, with at least four members, could act as a court of chancery, to hear and decide all cases in equity.[2]

The council was a legislative as well as an executive body, and no act could be passed unless it gave its assent. As the upper house it kept its own journals, and these give abundant evidence that this body bore a very important part in the law-making of the prov-

[1] C. R. III, 405–10, 412, 414, 417, 421, 425; IV, 2, 33, 233–34, 461–62; V, 828, 1017; VI, 330–31, 758, 773, 1009.
[2] C. R. III, 204, 251, 425, 428; VI, 1009, 1017; VII, 5; VIII, 269–70.

ince. In practically all matters it had equal rights, powers and privileges with the lower house; in some points it had greater powers. The upper house alone could declare a bill rejected or order it engrossed by the lower house; and all bills must pass both houses, through three readings, receive a majority vote in each and be engrossed before they could go to the governor for his signature. Either house could make amendments to the other's bills. Frequent conferences of the two houses were held over the amendments; sometimes they came to an agreement, but very often did not. When no agreement could be reached, the upper house declared the bill for which the amendments had been proposed and not accepted rejected. This right of rejecting all bills to which it could not assent was very frequently exercised by the upper house, and gave it considerable influence. And the council in a semi-legislative capacity at times advised the governor to assent to or reject bills which had passed both houses.[1] In its executive capacity it advised the governor to prorogue, dissolve, or call the assembly, and such advice was as a rule acted upon by the governor.[2] The council had, therefore, a two-fold law-making function, one as an executive and the other as a purely legislative body. When it was determined to do so, it could block or hinder any legislation, in spite of the demands of the governor and the lower house, but the lower house could in reality do the same. As a rule, however, it was in sympathy with the position of the chief

[1] C. R. III–IX, passim.
[2] C. R. III, 415, 536; IV, 461; V, 34; VII, 752; VIII, 37, 150.

executive in his attempts to secure the passage of certain acts. The councillors, like the governor, were agents of the crown, and in exercising their law-making powers they for the most part entertained ideas similar to his.

It is difficult to estimate exactly how efficient the council as an executive body was. The records seem to point to the conclusion that upon the whole this body was not very efficient, though its policy was to support the home government. Under Burrington it did little but dispute over personal or constitutional matters. Under Johnston, Dobbs and Tryon, there was practical agreement between it and the governor, though not the greatest possible efficiency. Martin's relations with this department of the government were not very pleasant and harmonious. By 1772 the councillors had begun to see the drift of affairs in the American colonies, that all was tending to oppose the English administration, and they took sides with the colonists in several of their demands.[1] While the full number was twelve, still only a very few times did all of them ever meet in one council. They lived in different parts of the province, had many personal interests to look after, and received little or no allowance.[2] It was, therefore, most natural that they should not take a very great or profound interest in the government of the province. This part of the executive was less efficient than the governor. The councillors were colonists and did not feel themselves to be under strict

[1] C. R. III–IX, passim.
[2] C. R. III–IX, passim.

responsibility to the crown; they might be suspended from office for neglect, but this penalty was of little consequence to them. The governor on the other hand was the special agent of the crown and was directly responsible to it. He was a citizen of Great Britain, not a colonist. It was his duty to govern the province in the best possible way, and removal from office meant far more to him than it did to a councillor.

As we have seen, the governor was instructed to act with no less than five members, unless in cases of great emergency, when he might allow three to constitute a quorum for business.[1] As the records indicate, a good many meetings were held in which only three were present, and the governor by force of circumstances was compelled to act with these. In November, 1741, a council met in which nine out of the twelve were present,[2] but this was the largest meeting between 1731 and 1742. At the meetings between 1754 and 1775 seven councillors were frequently present. Whether the number was large or small, many of the meetings in an executive capacity were wholly of a routine nature, and much business of this kind was disposed of without great attention or care. When acting in a legislative capacity the council as a rule showed much more vigor and intelligence, and the number at the meetings of this nature was larger than at the executive sessions. It was in service of this kind that the council contributed the most to the interest and welfare of the royal government.

[1] C. R. III, 91–93.
[2] C. R. IV, 587.

Concerning their general relations with the governor much can be said both to their credit and discredit. Under Burrington the council as an executive body could not act in harmony with the governor. The meetings were frequently small and were made up chiefly of those councillors who held other offices—that of chief justice or secretary. These officers were selfish and looked after interests of their own and consequently came easily into conflict with the governor. Burrington, in a report to Secretary Newcastle, July, 1731, stated that he had been involved in a great debate with three of the council—Smith, Ashe and Edmund Porter—over the powers of the assistant justices; that he had claimed that the assistant justices had some judicial powers independent of the chief justice, but that Chief Justice Smith and his two allies mentioned above claimed that the assistant justices were only the mere supporters of the chief justice.[1] With this report he sent papers in which he claimed that the said three councillors named above would not attend the meetings though duly summoned, because they did not agree with his opinion in regard to the powers of the assistant justices.[2] During September of the same year he wrote to the board of trade to the effect that some of the councillors offered more obstruction to his administration than did the lower house. He stated that when he had called a council to nominate a chief justice in the place of Smith, who had left the province, only Jenoure and Porter appeared, and that the

[1] C. R. III, 150, 233, 236–38.
[2] C. R. III, 168–75.

other councillors were either out of the province or at
Cape Fear, two hundred miles away. He further said
that he then asked the two present about appointing
others, so that there might be a sufficient number with
which to hold a chancery court; that Jenoure readily
assented to it, but that Porter would not;[1] that he was
compelled by the circumstances to swear in for the
time two others in order to appoint a chief justice and
hold a court of chancery.[2] But his opponents in the
council denied that they had hindered the cause of
good government by their demands and conduct, and
declared that Burrington by his arbitrary and illegal
acts had done so.[3] The evidence when analyzed shows
that, while Burrington was arbitrary and uncompromising, he was not to a great extent illegal or unconstitutional in his position, and that the councillors were
certainly as much responsible as the governor for their
failure to serve the crown.[4]

Under Johnston, both as an executive and a legislative body, the council acted in substantial agreement
with the governor and among themselves. At several
times during his administration they assured him that
they would do all in their power to be in accord with
his wishes and the crown's interests. But still this
department of the government was by no means very
efficient. He, in writing to the board of trade in 1740,
stated that there were four vacancies in the council,

[1] C. R. III, 196–97.
[2] C. R. III, 207–210.
[3] C. R. III, 386–88.
[4] C. R. III, 370–82, 429–38, 559, 625–27.

and that two of them were due to the fact that two of those appointed by the crown in 1730 had never come to the province.[1] The board of trade in 1752 made an investigation concerning the council and found that there were then only three persons in it whom the crown had appointed.[2] This is one bit of evidence, out of very much, that the authorities in England paid little attention to the composition and efficiency of this body.

The relations of the council with Dobbs were pleasant, but their efficiency under him was certainly not of a high grade. He informed the authorities in England that some of the councillors never attended a meeting unless it was held at or near their own homes,[3] and also that at times he could not hold an assembly because of a lack of a sufficient number of the council to constitute the upper house.[4] It was during his administration that an attempt was made by the home government to pay the councillors for their expenses while sitting in an executive or judicial capacity, but this attempt was apparently never successful, even under the later governors.[5] To avoid some abuses which had occurred rather frequently, Dobbs, in 1761, laid before the council one of his instructions from the crown, which forbade the governor to allow the councillors as a legislative body any protection other than of their

[1] C. R. IV, 81, 82, 114, 231, 425.
[2] C. R. IV, 1315.
[3] C. R. V, 439–41.
[4] C. R. VI, 243–44.
[5] C. R. V, 788; VI, 718–20; IX, 375.

persons, and that only during the session, and also prohibited their adjournment otherwise than *de die in diem* excepting on Sundays and holidays.[1]

The relations between Tryon and the council were harmonious to a great degree.[2] He, in writing to Secretary Hillsborough in 1769, stated that the councillors had acted well and uniformly for the crown's interest.[3] Martin and the council agreed upon most matters from 1771 to 1772, but after 1772 the councillors were disposed to take sides with the people in their opposition to the royal prerogative which he was attempting to compel them to accept and abide by. In April, 1774, he wrote to Secretary Dartmouth that the conduct of the council at the last session of the legislature was opposed to his administration, that it was unbecoming and tended to injure the interests of the crown.[4] He and the councillors had some difference of opinion on the bill for superior courts. The governor thought the bill was contrary to his instructions and that it encroached on the king's rights, but five of the councillors advised him to ratify it as the best possible measure under the circumstances.[5] He again wrote to Dartmouth, in May, 1775, that the conduct of the council had been very bad and disobedient.[6] In both instances he was speaking of the council as the upper house. He made no complaints of the council

[1] C. R. VI, 655–56.
[2] C. R. VII, 45–46, 554–55, 894; VIII, 100, 153, 290.
[3] C. R. VIII, 152–53.
[4] C. R. IX, 969–75.
[5] C. R. IX, 975–80.
[6] C. R. IX, 1242–45.

as an executive body, and one may conclude, therefore, that under him it discharged its routine executive duties in a fairly satisfactory manner.

The personal composition of the council was a matter in which the home authorities and governor were supposed to be much interested. To have an efficient council it was necessary to appoint the ablest and best men among the colonists as councillors. In this the governor had a large share. It was his duty to keep a list of the best men and of their qualifications before the crown and board of trade, from which they should choose in case of a vacancy. Upon the whole the governor showed intelligence in discharging his duty; a good many of his recommendations and nominations were wise and expedient. The king and board of trade, in making the final choice, were in the main influenced by what the governor had to say, though frequently they did not heed his recommendations.

Among those who served the crown and province as councillors, and who are worthy of mention, were William Smith, Nathaniel Rice, John Baptiste Ashe, Eliezer Allen, Matthew Rowan, Cornelius Harnett, Roger Moore, Edward Moseley, Cullen Pollock, James Murray, William Forbes, James Hassell, James Innes, John Rutherford, John Swann, James Craven, Lewis DeRossett, Richard Spaight, H. E. McCulloh, Alexander McCulloh, Charles Berry, B. Heron, Marmaduke Jones and Thomas McGuire.[1] These were men of influence and ability. They lived in different parts of

C. R. III, 91, 209; IV, 1, 3, 31, 445, 1315; V, 817; VI, 559; VII, 137; IX, 52, 1207; State Records I, 126, 146–47.

the province and knew the conditions of their several localities. They understood the position of the crown, as they were its agents, and likewise the standpoint of the colonists among whom they lived.

The council, though it was not a very efficient body in its executive capacity, still in the main contributed much to the good government of the province. It was in the main a body composed of men of ability, intelligence and honesty. It exercised a beneficent restraint upon the lower house of the legislature, prevented the governor from making many mistakes, and brought respect and dignity to the royal government.

CHAPTER IV.

THE LOWER HOUSE OF THE LEGISLATURE UNDER THE CROWN.

The position of the executive—the governor and the council—has already been considered, and their powers, duties and acts discussed. The functions of the council as the upper house of the legislature have likewise been under consideration. It now remains to consider the other branch of the legislature—the lower house. This, like the governor and the council, was in existence when North Carolina became a royal province. It was provided for in the charters of 1663 and 1665, which the crown gave to the proprietors, and they by their instructions to their governors gave orders as to its qualifications and workings. When the province became royal the lower house was provided for in the commissions and instructions from the crown to the royal governors. The crown was now the direct and immediate source of the provincial laws, but it, like the proprietors, delegated many of the law-making powers to the general assembly, of which the lower house was an important part.

The organization and privileges of this body were defined, to a large extent, by the instructions to the governor; many of its privileges came at the will of the crown and, therefore, did not belong to it inherently or from proprietary grants, as it was at times strongly disposed to claim. The fact, however, that this body had been in legal and actual existence for more than fifty years entitled it to some privileges independent of the crown. But still the crown gave it few privileges of a positive nature, most of the instructions pertaining to the lower house being of the nature of prohibitions. The governor was ordered to see that the members of this branch of the legislature were chosen by the freeholders only, and he was forbidden to allow them any protection other than of their persons during the session, or to allow them to adjourn without his leave otherwise than *de die in diem,* except on Sundays and holidays. He was instructed to see that the council had like powers with the lower house in framing money bills, and that all enacting clauses should be in the name of the governor, council and lower house. In short, he could not allow the assembly any rights or privileges which custom had not permitted to the house of commons in England.[1]

He was also instructed not to allow any act or ordinance for levying money, imposing fines and penalties, unless with a clause which expressly stated that they were for the crown and the benefit of the province; and he could permit no act by which the crown's revenue might be lessened or impaired without royal permission. He was ordered to see that all laws for the support of the government were for an unlimited time, excepting those for purely temporary purposes. He could not assent to acts of an extraordinary nature,

[1] C. R. III, 93–94.

whereby the royal prerogative, the property of English subjects and the trade of Great Britain, might be affected, until he had transmitted draughts of the same to the crown and received the royal approval, unless the said acts contained clauses suspending their execution until the crown's pleasure was known; nor could he assent to laws for a shorter time than two years, except those imposing taxes on wines and liquors, and these must be of at least twelve months' duration. He was not permitted to reënact any laws which had been disallowed by the crown, unless with its special leave, nor could he assent to any act which repealed any law then in force unless it contained a clause suspending its execution until the authorities in England passed upon it. He was also ordered not to assent to any private act whereby the property of any person would be effected, in which there was no clause saving the rights of the crown, those of all bodies politic and corporate, and of all other persons not mentioned in the act.[1]

The lower house during the whole of the royal period claimed that it had some rights, inherent in its own nature and derived from the proprietors, which the crown must allow. By an act of 1715–1716 it had ordered that assemblies should be held biennially in spite of what the proprietors desired. This act also regulated the elections, the qualifications of the voters and of the representatives. Whether the proprietors accepted this act or not, and this is a debated question, is of little importance in this connection; the colonists

[1] C. R. III, 93–96, 496–98; V, 1103–44; VII, 137–42; VIII, 512–16.

exercised the rights and claimed the privileges of it from 1716 to 1731. Burrington in 1731 advised the crown to repeal it for the reason that it was contrary to the principles laid down in his instructions from the crown; and apparently it was repealed by the crown, though at what time is not known. The fact that Burrington in 1731 was ordered by the king to hold elections according to the principles of his instructions is evidence that the crown then meant that the act of 1715–1716 was no longer binding. Still an act was passed by the assembly, assented to by Johnston and allowed by the crown in 1734, repealing a clause in the said act of 1715–1716, and in 1743 an act was passed and agreed to which repealed the act of 1734. These two acts of 1734 and 1743 are good evidence that the lower house under the crown did exercise some rights in regulating its privileges, even independently of the crown, as the act of 1743 regulated the elections of the members of the lower house and defined the qualifications of the members and of the electors. This act was in operation in 1752. In 1760 another act was assented to by the chief executive and allowed by the crown to substantially the same effect, and this was in operation in 1765.[1]

One of the privileges which the lower house claimed was that of determining the suffrage. As to what this was during the whole royal period we can not say with great accuracy. The royal government began with the principle of freehold suffrage, and this appears to have been the case during the larger part, if not all, of the

[1] Swann, 79; Davis, 1765, II, 198–201; C. R. III, 180–81.

period.[1] The records would indicate that the assembly, while it passed certain acts defining the qualifications of voters, did so for the most part according to the instructions from the crown, which insisted upon freehold suffrage. To be a freeholder in North Carolina, however, was not very difficult, and consequently suffrage was not greatly limited. The lower house also claimed the privilege of making inquiries into the election returns of its own members.[2] At an assembly in July, 1733, several representatives appeared from the new precincts of Onslow, Bladen and Edgecombe, but the lower house refused to admit them until it had made an investigation as to whether these precincts had the legal right to send representatives. A conference was held between the two houses on this matter, and it was agreed that the precincts could send members to the next session of the assembly.[3] The lower house also declared that the governor and council alone did not have the right of erecting new precincts, that they must be erected by the consent of the lower house as well. On this ground it had refused to admit the representatives from the above named precincts, which had been erected by the governor and council without the consent of itself.[4]

The question of the number of representatives from each precinct or county was of great importance and at times brought on much discussion. The first lower

[1] C. R. III, 93, 497; V, 1110–11; VII, 137–42; VIII, 512–16.
[2] C. R. III, 288–89.
[3] C. R. III, 581–83.
[4] C. R. III, 575–76.

house under Burrington had representatives as follows: five each from Chowan, Perquimans, Pasquotank, Bertie; four from Currituck; two each from Beaufort, Hyde, Craven, Carteret; one each from the towns of Edenton, Newbern, Bath.[1] There was never any discussion about the right of each town, which had a certain population, to send one delegate to the assembly. But there was a long struggle between the young counties, which could send only two, and the older counties, which had the privilege of five representatives. The older counties were in the Albemarle or northeastern section. The people of this section were in much better circumstances than those in the southern or western counties; they had different social, economic and political ideas. To give the counties of the northeast five representatives each, while all the other counties had only two each, gave the control in matters of legislation to the more wealthy and aristocratic class. From one point of view this was an injustice, but it must be remembered that the older counties had a larger population and many more vested interests than the new counties. Governor Johnston, urged on by what he thought to be a great injustice, and by the fact that he could not control the representatives from Albemarle as easily as he desired, made several attempts to do away with this unequal representation in the lower house. His earlier attempts failed because of the control which the large representation gave to the older counties. He desired to bring about a system of equal representation from each county, whether

[1] C. R. III, 285.

old or new, large or small. But this was impossible in an assembly in which the Albemarle counties had a large majority. He, being convinced that the only way to accomplish his object was by moving the provincial capital to the extreme southern part of the province, called an assembly to meet in the town of Wilmington in 1746. To this assembly the representatives of the northeastern counties would not go, as Wilmington was more than two hundred miles away and almost a wilderness separated it from Albemarle. By this assembly, which really represented only the southern and southwestern counties, an act was passed which provided for two representatives from each county and one from each town. This act also provided that eight members could adjourn *de die in diem* until as many as fourteen and the speaker, who could constitute a quorum, arrived. This provision was necessary to carry out the idea of equal representation.[1] The act of 1746 was in operation until 1754, when the crown repealed it.[2] From 1746 to 1754 the counties of the northeast had no representation in the lower house, as they would not send any delegation smaller than their customary number—five. But from 1754 to 1775 the representation was unequal as it had been previous to 1746.[3]

Governor Dobbs was instructed, in 1754, to erect towns and counties in the southern and western part of the province whenever he and the council deemed it

[1] Swann, 223–24.
[2] C. R. V, 1110–11.
[3] C. R. V, 231–32; VI–IX, passim.

fit. He was to do this, not by an act of the assembly, but by charters of incorporation which gave the said towns and counties the privilege of sending representatives to the lower house.[1] This right of the governor was denied by many of the colonists, and it appears that Dobbs was not able to carry out fully his intentions concerning this, at least for some time after his administration began. In March, 1759, it was ordered by the council that the governor issue a proclamation to the effect that, upon the dissolution of the assembly then elected, no writs of election could be issued to several counties and towns unless they took out charters of incorporation from the governor.[2] This would indicate that several towns and counties had been sending representatives without receiving the right to do so from the governor. But still Dobbs had exercised his right of granting charters of incorporation in 1757.[3] After 1759 the right of representation apparently depended upon the charters of incorporation issued by the governor; the colonists gave up their claims in the matter.[4]

The lower house was elected according to writs from the governor, and the members must take from him the oaths of allegiance and supremacy to the crown.[5] He prorogued and dissolved it whenever he and the council saw fit, and this was done very frequently. In his

[1] C. R. V, 1111.
[2] C. R. VI, 77.
[3] C. R. V, 767–68.
[4] C. R. VIII, 251, 543.
[5] C. R. III, 66–73.

opening speeches at the beginning of each session he outlined his policy to the representatives, spoke of their rights and duties, and made his requests. He allowed them to choose their own speaker and clerk, to keep their journals, to originate, discuss and amend bills, but the final rejection of a bill was in the power of the council and himself. By virtue of the fact that the lower house had control of the supplies, it compelled the governor not infrequently to assent to its demands, and in so doing it exercised a very considerable influence over him and his administration. While he and the council could reject any bill which the lower house passed, still they could never pass any act unless the lower house gave its assent. This gave it the power of forcing the governor and council to allow it to have and to exercise a good many general and special privileges, to which it was not entitled by written law.

Such were the privileges of the lower house. It also had certain specified powers, some of which the crown gave by voluntary grant, while others came to it by custom or by assumption. Along with the powers were their correlative duties. The lower house had and exercised considerable powers in regulating the territorial system, especially in excusing the colonists from the penalties of non-compliance with the regulations. The governor and council had control of the greater part of the administration of this system, but the lower house had at least its share in the passing of the territorial laws, which the chief executive was instructed to secure. During the royal period seventeen acts concerning land were passed by the assembly and agreed to by the governor and crown. These acts were concerning the proper settlement and cultivation, enrolling and registering, titles, rent-rolls and quit-rents, and the relief of those who failed to comply with the laws and regulations.[1] The crown gave directions to the governor in regard to some of the general regulations of the system, but it was left to the governor and assembly to work out all the details of the administration. A careful analysis of these details as shown in the laws furnishes much evidence that the lower house had more than its constitutional share, certainly so in view of the interpretation which the crown officers placed upon this constitution. Not only did it take a leading part in passing the acts, but it also made many complaints to the governor about the granting of lands at high rents, about the inconvenience of the places where rents were paid and about the dishonesty of the collectors. In fact its members exercised a general supervision over the administration of the whole system,[2] a right which the crown had reserved for the governor and the council. They went so far as to maintain that all lands should be granted to the colonists at the very low rates as specified in the grant of 1668, which they were fond of calling the "original deed."[3]

With the general administration of the province the

---

[1] Swann, 85, 90, 138, 155, 275, 285, 329; Davis, 1765, II, 35, 70, 82, 211, 331; Davis, 1773, 344, 464, 491, 560, 562.

[2] C. R. III–IX, passim.

[3] C. R. III, 289–93.

lower house had much to do. It acted jointly with the
upper house in inspecting and settling all public claims
and accounts. It ordered the public treasurers to lay
all their accounts before it and often appointed and
controlled them, attempted to ascertain and regulate
the fees of all officers, in what they should be paid and
at what rates, complained of the bad conduct of officers
and of the lack of courts, made addresses to the governor and crown concerning the laws, currency, trade,
lands, rents and tenants of the province, and appointed
and controlled for the most part an agent who resided
in England. The governor in his opening speeches
encouraged much of this and asked the representatives
to promote the welfare of the province by establishing
a good system of trade, religion and education.[1] This
request of the governor gave them a legal right to look
after the general administration in several matters;
other rights they assumed as belonging to themselves
by virtue of the fact that they were the representatives
of the people who were governed and who paid the
taxes. The chief among these rights were the appointment and control of the treasurers. The governor was
much opposed to this claim and declared that the lower
house in making it was assuming to regulate the executive and was, therefore, taking away from him his constitutional rights.[2] But in spite of the protest on the
part of the executive, the lower house in the main
appointed and controlled the treasurers.

The lower house had its share in passing the acts

[1] C. R. III, 269, 277, 291, 294, 542; IV–IX, passim.
[2] C. R. VI, 1253.

for the militia and defence. In the eight militia acts
passed by the assembly and allowed by the crown the
interests of the colonists were considered as much, if
not more than, those of the crown. The governor
urged that some of them be enacted and suggested
changes in others. The acts also show the influence
of the lower house. The general form of these laws
was in conformity with the English models, but in the
details there was much that was distinctly provincial
and of the North Carolina type.[1] It was the lower
house especially to which the governor applied for soldiers, arms, supplies and forts, either for defensive or
offensive war. This was done in 1740, and the lower
house readily granted Johnston a considerable number
of soldiers and all the supplies required for them,
though these were to aid England in carrying on an offensive war against the Spanish West Indies.[2] From
1754 to 1762 the governor had to make many requests
for troops and money with which to defend the province and to aid its neighbors, and as a rule the assembly complied with his requests. By 1760 it had
granted a considerable number of soldiers and about
80,000 pounds to the common cause of the colonies,[3]
and it continued to grant aid, though not large, until
the war was ended and all danger was removed.[4] The
lower house also took a prominent part in suppressing
the insurrection of the "regulators" in 1768–1771.[5]

[1] Law Revisals, passim.
[2] C. R. IV, 550–55.
[3] C. R. VI, 476–78.
[4] C. R. VI, 803, 808–10, 831, 1090; VII, 552.
[5] C. R. VII, 926–27; VIII, 333, 385.

While the governor was given full military powers and could, therefore, theoretically exercise them without consulting the legislature, still he could in reality do nothing without the sympathy and aid of this department of the government. He must have soldiers and money, and in order to secure these he had to give up many of his powers to the lower house which alone could really grant them. So that the lower house, while in theory it had few military powers, exercised great influence over military affairs.

In judicial matters this body exercised considerable powers. It made resolves about the proper or improper way of administering justice, and with the upper house it decided on jurymen for the counties; it might and did at times request the governor to pardon those guilty of violating the laws of the province. It also had its part in passing the acts which erected courts. And in most of the bills erecting courts the lower house attempted to insert clauses dealing with the qualifications and time of service of the judges, the amount and extent of the jurisdiction of the different courts, and foreign attachments, all of which clauses were considered by the crown as assumptions on the part of the lower house, contrary to English custom and law.[1] These claims the executive for the most part opposed, inasmuch as they were contrary to the principles of his instructions, and the crown stood by its governor in this. Neither would the lower house give up its claims, and, therefore, no compromise was ever reached.

[1] C. R. III, 587–90, 603–40; IV, 515–25, 488; VI, 802–04; IX, 169, 173.

7

And, lastly, the lower house had a large part in the passing of acts for the government of the province. However, in this, as in all its other powers, there were many limitations upon the lower house. The fact that the governor and council had the power to call for a new election, adjourn, prorogue and dissolve the lower house, is evidence of how subordinate was the theoretical position of this body in law-making. But when once called it had about one third of the law-making powers within its control. All bills had to be passed through three readings and receive a majority vote in each house before the governor could assent to them. While the upper house always had the right to order a bill engrossed by the lower house, or to reject any bill to which it could not assent, still the lower house had in reality the same right. The governor had full power of assenting to or rejecting the bills passed by both houses, and also of proroguing or dissolving the assembly when he thought it was going too far in its discussions and claims.[1]

The lower house, however, in actual practice had far more than its theoretical powers. The governor and the upper house frequently were compelled by circumstances to allow it certain powers and the passage of certain acts, which were really contrary to English customs and the governor's instructions, in order to secure any bill at all for the government or any money for the expenses thereof in time of peace or war. A careful study of the laws passed during the royal period and of the method of their passage reveals the

[1] C. R. III–IX, passim; Law Revisals, passim.

great power which the lower house at many times had. In many different ways it compelled the upper house and the governor to assent to its bills, though against royal instructions. It represented the people who paid the money and fought the battles of the royal government, and as such had very great powers.[1]

Concerning the efficiency of the lower house during the whole period of royal government few accurate statements can be made. Under Burrington no bills became laws. Who was to blame it is difficult to say with exactness. The evidence, as far as it exists, shows that both the governor and the lower house were extreme and uncompromising in their demands.[2] For the most part the lower house was obedient to the requests of Johnston, and many bills were agreed to by him.[3] With Dobbs it was on good terms until 1760, when his continued, though necessary, requests for soldiers and money caused it to find fault with his administration and to refuse his requests.[4] Tryon, by his diplomatic ways, had no difficulty with the representatives and secured their sympathy and aid in almost all of his undertakings.[5] Martin had to meet them at a very critical time. The fiscal and judicial problems had

[1] C. R. III–IX, passim; Law Revisals, passim.

[2] C. R. III, 257–325, 541, 549–52, 636–38.

[3] C. R. IV, 77–79, 83–85, 243, 380–414, 418, 549–51, 771–72, 777–78, 834–38, 863–67.

[4] C. R. V, 309–10, 558–59, 734–36, 924, 1010–11; VI, 99, 138–40, 369–72, 425, 467–69, 511, 695, 811, 835–37, 1024, 1036.

[5] C. R. VII, 43, 60–61, 63–64, 291–92, 347–49, 355–56, 421, 423, 550, 552, 569–70, 624, 668–70; VIII, 104–05, 140–41, 284–86, 311–13, 383–84, 477–79, 492–94.

now become very grave. He was a prerogative governor and they a democratic house. The natural consequences were that they could not agree.[1]

The acts of the legislature and the part which the lower house took in their passage give very abundant evidence of the honesty and sincerity of the representatives of the people. To be sure they took extreme positions at times, as against the governor and council; they laid claims to privileges and rights to which they were not constitutionally entitled; they followed an unsound and unjust fiscal policy, but this was more a question of judgment than of intention. With it all they did many things for the support and welfare of the royal government in the province, and were loyal subjects of the king. They watched the interests of the colonists and defended them against what they deemed to be encroachments on the part of the royal officials, and this they had the inherent right to do. The lower house had among its members several men of fine intelligence and ability. While as a whole body it was not so distinguished for ability as the council, still in devotion to what they believed to be their duty they were excelled by none.

[1] C. R. IX, 101, 221–22, 346, 373–74, 442–45, 476–77, 583–87, 707–09, 737–43, 787–88, 790–91, 874–76, 879–80, 927–28, 945–46, 955, 1188–95, 1205.

CHAPTER V.

The Territorial System and Administration.

The more formal powers and duties of the executive and legislature, and how they were in a general way executed and discharged, have been under consideration. It remains to consider in their practical workings the policies and acts of the executive and the crown, of the legislature and the colonists, upon questions arising from land, money, justice and defence.

The territorial system under any form of government is of fundamental importance, especially so in a pioneer community. In North Carolina, whether under the proprietors or the crown, the system and the policy concerning land determined to a very considerable extent the economic, social and political life of the colonists. The colonial history of North Carolina was very different in many respects from that of Virginia or South Carolina, her neighbors, not so much because her people were so different, as in reality they were not, but chiefly because of the different policies concerning land and the methods of granting it. Had the crown exercised the chief control in the government of the two Carolinas from their settlement, as it did in Virginia from 1624, it is probable that these three provinces would have had substantially the same territorial system and policy. However, while the Carolinas were under the same patentees, and these were guided by the principles of their charters from the crown, still they had two distinct policies in regard to the territorial administration, though only one general system.

While this study is concerned chiefly with the royal period, still it is absolutely necessary to consider, briefly at least, the system and its effects under the proprietors. When, in 1729, the crown by purchase from the patentees became the owner of seven-eighths of the whole Carolina grant, it introduced few changes in the system then established. The chief difference was in its administration; the crown attempted to make it much more efficient than it had previously been. All the grants made by the proprietors were declared by the crown to be valid, and most of the laws concerning land which were in force prior to 1729 were allowed to be reenacted with slight changes or to continue in operation without any changes whatever. The principles of the charters to the proprietors were still regarded as the legal basis of land-holding.

The proprietors had many powers over their land, but all of these came to them from their charters. They formulated the system in its details and provided for its execution, but in accord with the general principles as laid down by the crown. By their charters the patentees became feudal seigniors, having control of both the land and the government, under certain conditions and limitations. But they held their lands from the crown in free and common socage tenure, not by knight's service, paying a merely nominal rent—one-fourth of the gold and silver mined and twenty marks yearly.[1] This merely nominal rent, however, was a full recognition of the fact that the crown still remained the ultimate owner of the lands. Though feudal seigniors, they were not placed under all of the restrictions laid upon such persons during the later feudal times in England. The principle of *quia emptores,* as established for England by 18 Edward I., which forbade subinfeudation, was not to apply to the Carolinas. This gave the patentees the authority to establish a system of feudal tenants in their province. The proprietors, their heirs and assigns, could assign, grant or demise their lands to any person whatsoever; and this could be done by a title in fee simple, fee tail or for years. They also had the power of determining upon the rents of such lands, as they deemed best.[2] The tenants of the patentees, however, were also under the control of the crown in many particulars; they were always to be subjects of the crown, and were also entitled to the same civil and property rights as Englishmen.[3]

Being thus empowered, the proprietors announced to those who would become colonists the conditions under which they could have and hold land. The first statement of these conditions was made during 1663 in a document entitled "the declaration and proposals."[4] By this they offered to issue grants under the free and

[1] C. R. I, 104.
[2] C. R. I, 28–29.
[3] C. R. I, 106–07.
[4] C. R. I, 43–46.

common socage tenure, to the grantee and his heirs
forever. With the view of encouraging a rapid settlement, they offered special inducements to large families. These lands were not sold, but leased forever, as
it were. At first there was no cash payment upon taking up lands; the proprietors were paid in the shape
of an annual quit-rent. This system of quit-rents was
established at once after the patentees obtained their
charters,[1] and by means of it they retained the ultimate control of all their lands. It was of decided
advantage to poor colonists; they could become colonists and take up lands without advancing any money.
One half-penny per acre was the amount established
by the proprietors as the quit-rent, and from three to
five years were allowed for its payment. However,
lands were granted during 1663 at a lower rate than
this, only one farthing per acre being called for;[2] and
this very low rate, being chiefly to attract a large number of colonists, was approved by the patentees in their
second document of conditions according to which
lands were to be granted, that of 1665, and again in
their "original deed" of 1668.[3]

Beginning with 1667, many of the powers and duties
pertaining to lands were transferred by the patentees
to the provincial officers. The assembly, of which the
governor was a part, was now to prescribe the quan-
tity of land to be granted to any one person, and likewise to make the rules for the administration of the

[1] C. R. I, 46, 51–52.
[2] C. R. I, 51–52, 55, 59–67.
[3] C. R. I, 88, 89, 92, 175–76, 181–83.

land office. Such a transfer of powers, however, was
by no means final, and was also subject to many limitations; while the assembly had a part to perform in
the territorial policy and administration, still this was
done in the main according to specific instructions from
the patentees. Nevertheless, the assembly enacted
several laws concerning land, and most of these were
approved by the proprietors.[1]   In 1669 three such acts
were passed, and they were confirmed by the patentees
during the next year. One of these determined the
size of the grant to any one person, and thereby
modified the provisions of the "fundamental constitutions" concerning land, which the patentees issued during the same year. The constitutions looked toward
making very large grants, while the said act of the
assembly allowed only six hundred and sixty acres to
any one colonist. Another act provided for a speedy
settlement of the grants; and a third required that a
person should be an inhabitant of the province for at
least two years before he could dispose by sale of his
rights to lands.[2]   The fact that these three acts were
passed by the assembly and confirmed by the proprietors is strong evidence that both parties now desired
to establish in North Carolina a system of small holdings. The patentees, however, had a different system
in their minds, which was to be put in operation some
time in the future.[3]

In 1679 the proprietors began to make changes in

[1] C. R. I, 169, 175–76, 181–83.
[2] C. R. I, 184–86.
[3] C. R. I, 187–206.

the system. Quit-rents were raised from one half-
penny to one penny per acre; and lands were to be settled within one year in the place of three as at first
required. These changes, of course, did not affect the
grants already made and not forfeited.[1] Further
changes were made in 1694. Now the governor and
at least three deputies of the proprietors, advising together, could sell lands in fee, demanding as high a
purchase price as they saw fit, with the one limitation
that no lands could be sold for less than ten pounds
per one thousand acres. This sale was not a wholly
unqualified one, as five shillings per one thousand acres
should be reserved as the annual rent.[2] This was the
beginning of a new system — a combination of the purchase and the lease systems. By means of this change
the patentees received more money at the time of the
sale and less in the shape of annual quit-rents, and
apparently it was kept up during the remaining years
of the proprietary government.[3]

From the years 1712–1713 the assembly had much
more to do with the system and its administration than
it had previously had. The proprietors now began to
entrust more and more to the provincial officers, and
sent out few specific instructions in regard to land, as
well as other matters. In 1713 the provincial officers
and the legislature began to take a much more active
and intelligent interest in their political and economic
affairs. They now by an act regulated with more care

[1] C. R. I, 59–67, 237–38.
[2] C. R. I, 390–92; IV, 308–15.
[3] C. R. I, 556, 696, 707, 846; IV, 308–15.

the conditions of purchasing lands, also provided that titles to lands already purchased should no longer be of force unless the purchase money was paid within three months after the passage of this act.[1]   The failure to pay this purchase money had been very common, and was, therefore, very annoying to the proprietors and their officers in the province.   Again, during 1715–1716, the assembly legislated upon territorial matters; it now made a revisal of all the laws concerning land which had previously been in force and which it now desired should continue in operation, with greater or less modification.   This revisal contained unchanged two of the acts of 1669–1670, on the transfer of rights and on the speedy settlement, and many other regulations.   The assembly declared valid all former grants and enacted that seven years quiet possession under the color of a claim gave a good title; it also determined upon the conditions and methods of escheat, regulated the abuses in the taking up and the surveying of lands, and defined the limits of time in which the purchase money should be paid.   Not only were these provisions passed by the assembly and confirmed by the patentees, but they were also allowed to continue in force far into the royal period.[2]   This revisal, to an extent of new provisions, but to a larger extent of old ones reënacted, supplemented by an act concerning titles to lands passed during 1723,[3] was the legal basis of granting, holding and administering the lands dur-

[1] C. R. II, 173.
[2] C. R. I, 184, 186; MS. Laws; Swann, 7–13.
[3] Swann, 54.

ing the later years of the proprietary period and to a
considerable extent throughout the period of the royal
administration.

The proprietors had a fairly definite method of
granting, surveying and registering lands. However,
in as much as this was not very different from that
under the crown, nothing will be said of it in this connection except to the effect that more abuses occurred
in its administration under the patentees than under
the royal officials. As to the size of the grants made
by the proprietors there was much uniformity; they
were for the most part small. The largest amount
granted to any one person was as a rule six hundred
and forty acres, but one who had a large family of
servants might obtain as much as seventeen hundred
acres. The patentees from the very first insisted upon
small holdings for the northern settlement, at least until they could establish a system of feudal lords upon
its lands. In 1670 the assembly enacted a law, which
they accepted, to the effect that six hundred and sixty
acres should be the largest grant issued to any one
person unless he were one of the proprietors, a land-
grave or a cassique. However, by the proprietors'
expressed permission much larger grants might be issued.[2] But early in the eighteenth century the policy
of small grants became quite well defined. In 1702
instructions were sent by the patentees to the governor
to the effect that no grants could be of more than six
hundred acres; and from 1712 to the end of their ad-

[1] C. R. I, 52, 72, 73, 165–75, 845–46; II, passim.
[2] C. R. I, 186.

ministration the proprietors instructed to the effect that all grants be limited to six hundred and forty acres.[1]

While the policy of making small grants was the usual one, still there were exceptions to it. Prior to 1670 a few grants were made with as many as eight hundred acres, and between 1711 and 1729 there are records of grants containing as many as five or ten thousand acres. But these large grants were very exceptional; six hundred and forty acres were the largest amount with the fewest exceptions from 1693 to 1729.[2] The policy of the proprietors toward North Carolina was in this particular very different from that of South Carolina; as a rule they issued small grants for the one, but quite large ones for the other. One of the results of such a policy was that the northern province became settled by many small and poor farmers, while the southern became the home of great holdings and of aristocratic ideas. Virginia was also the home of great plantations, and in this respect was unlike her neighbor to the south.

After experimenting with their province for more than fifty years, the patentees were willing and even anxious to surrender the powers and responsibilities of government and to sell the larger part of their lands. Their attempts at government, as we have seen, had been unsuccessful, and the profits from their investment had been very small. As early as 1719 the colonists of the southern province had overthrown their administration and accepted that of the crown. While

[1] C. R. I, 556, 846; II, 457.
[2] MS. Records of the Land Office.

those of the northern province gave no signs of such
action, still the patentees were not sure of their future
developments; they were ready to sell to the crown,
at least the larger part of their lands, and the crown,
as we have already seen, was desirous of obtaining a
more complete control over the Carolinas.[1] On or before July 11, 1728, negotiations for such a transfer
were concluded. The purchase price for the whole
grant was 25,000 pounds, 5,000 of which were for the
arrears of quit-rents still due the patentees.[2] However, this was not the end of the matter; an act was
passed by Parliament on or before June 1, 1729, which
completed the purchase. By this act only seven-
eighths of the original grant were surrendered to the
crown, Lord Carteret, afterwards Earl of Granville,
retaining one-eighth; and the price was 17,500 pounds
for the lands thus surrendered and 5,000 for the arrears of quit-rents due upon the whole grant.[3] The
crown now had entire control of the government, and
also was the owner of seven-eighths of the lands.

As has been stated, this transfer did not effect many
changes in the territorial system, policy or administration. All legal grants made by the proprietors were
confirmed by the crown, and their terms and conditions
were left unchanged. The crown also allowed the
same machinery of administration to continue in operation; the changes which were made were in the spirit
and policy rather than in the form.

[1] C. R. III, 6, 7, 10–12, 32–47.
[2] C. R. III, 6, 12; II, 769–70.
[3] C. R. III, 32–47.

Nothing was done toward laying off and bounding Carteret's share until 1743. During this year commissioners were appointed by the provincial officers, acting upon instructions from the crown, for the purpose of surveying and establishing the bounds of his portion. This portion, which was to be one-eighth of the whole of the original grant to the patentees, was located in one tract in the northern part of North Carolina. Of this tract the king in council made a formal grant to Carteret, September, 1744, in accordance with the provisions of the act of Parliament of 1729; and Carteret now executed a formal surrender of all his claims to the remaining portion. The formal grant of the king established as the boundaries of Carteret's lands the Virginia line on the north and latitude 35° 34' on the south. Over these lands Carteret was to be a feudal seignior of the crown, paying to it one-fourth of all the gold and silver mined upon his lands and a merely nominal yearly rent, of less than two pounds. In consequence of such a grant Carteret bore substantially the same relations to the crown as the original lords proprietors had done.[1]

This line of 35° 34' divided North Carolina into two almost equal parts; the original tract granted to the proprietors was far larger than the portion now embraced in the two Carolinas. Not only was Carteret's part almost one-half of the province, but it was decidedly the better half, being much older and more thickly settled. He was to receive all of the territorial revenue arising from his portion, quit-rents from the

[1] C. R. IV, 639, 655-63, 810-11; State Records I, 80-101.

lands already granted, and purchase money as well
as quit-rents from those to be granted; at the lowest
estimate he would receive at least one half of the
quit-rents of the whole province. This, of. course,
greatly diminished the crown's revenues in North
Carolina. The salaries of the crown officials must now
come from the quit-rents and purchase money obtained
from only one half of the province.

For his own lands Carteret put into operation a
territorial system, over which the crown had no control,[1] and this system was in form and policy much
like that which the original patentees had established.[2]
He was at its head; he appointed its agents, prescribed
its rules and dictated its policy. That he was far
sighted in the selection of his agents there is little evidence; that they did many illegal and fraudulent acts
there is an abundance of proof.[3] However, for the
first ten years his system worked without much fric-
tion. But from 1755 to 1760 there was much confusion and even a very considerable amount of disturbance. These became important enough for the lower
house of the legislature to take them under consideration; in 1755, after making some investigation into
them, it made complaints against the illegal acts of his
agents. While many of the charges made against his
agents were doubtless exaggerated and even false, still
apparently many of them were substantially true.
But to the complaints of the assembly Carteret, now

[1] C. R. V, 1106, 1134.
[2] Granville MS. Warrants, Indentures, Surveys.
[3] C. R. V–VIII, passim.

Earl of Granville, paid little heed, as he was not at all responsible to it. So many and strong were the complaints concerning the administration of his land office, that in 1758 a joint committee was appointed by the two houses of the legislature with full powers to make a thorough-going investigation. The investigation gave an abundance of evidence to the effect that the office was in a very deplorable condition and that his agents, Francis Corbin and Joshua Bodley, were both inefficient and dishonest. This was, however, the end of the matter. The legislature did nothing but make complaints and investigations; it had no power to do anything in the way of reforming the abuses.[1]

When the legislature, being powerless, failed to bring about reforms, the colonists in places assumed themselves the right of bringing relief to the deplorable state of affairs. Early in 1759 some of the people of Edgecombe County became riotous, seized Corbin, one of Granville's agents, placed him under heavy security to appear at the next court and render a full account of his official acts, especially of the fees which he had collected. Granville, either influenced by the complaints of the legislature or by this action on the part of the colonists, took steps toward bringing about reforms, though chiefly for his own protection against his agents. During April, 1759, he appointed Thomas Child as auditor of his agents.[2] Not only did the legislature complain of the administration of his terri-

[1] C. R. V, 299–300, 1089–94, 1017, 1042–43, 1050; VI, 21–22, 30, 312.

[2] C. R. VI, 21–22, 106–07.

8

torial system, but the governors also complained.
They strongly advised the crown to the effect that it
should obtain full control over Granville's lands by
purchasing them.[1] This opposition on the part of the
chief executive was due somewhat to the inefficiency
of the administration of the land office, but to a greater
extent to the fact that Granville obtained at least one
half of the revenues arising from all the lands in the
province, and thereby greatly diminished the sources
of the salaries of the crown officials.

Over the lands in North Carolina belonging to the
crown a royal land office was erected, but this, as has
been stated, was much the same as that under the original patentees. Not only did the crown confirm all the
legal grants made by the proprietors, but it also paid
off all of the quit-rents in arrears to them, the colonists no longer being held responsible for these. In
administering its system the crown, as the proprietors
had to a large extent done, recognized the rights of the
assembly; it advised the governor to secure acts from
the legislature whereby most matters relating to lands
should be regulated.[2] The crown reserved the right to
reject these whenever it deemed necessary. Not only
did it permit the assembly to pass new regulations, but
it also allowed many of the proprietary acts concerning land to continue in force, in some instances for
many years;[3] the system and policy of the proprietors
were not fundamentally changed.

[1] C. R. VI, 1022–25; VII, 154–57, 514–15; IX, 262, 580.
[2] C. R. III, 95, 101.
[3] C. R. III, 101–02, 497; V, 1105–06, 1127–34; VII, 137–42; VIII,
512–16; Swann, 7, 9, 10, 13, 54.

The land office under the crown had the following officers: the governor, council, secretary, surveyor-general, auditor, receiver-general, inspectors and commissioners of quit-rents, and the court of exchequer.

The powers and duties of the governor and council as officers of the territorial system have been under consideration in another connection. Here it is only necessary to state that they were at its head, having general oversight of its administration. They issued the warrants. These, being oftentimes signed by the secretary and auditor, as well as by the governor, were sent to the surveyor-general, who was thereby instructed to make the surveys and establish the boundaries of the lands as specified in the said warrants. A certificate of the surveys, with the warrants, must always be returned to the office of the chief executive or of the secretary. According to this certificate the governor or secretary issued a grant or patent, and this, when recorded in the office of the auditor, constituted a legal title.[1]

The secretary, of whom we have spoken, was one of the executive officers and was appointed by the crown. His duties were largely clerical, most of his attention being given to the land office.[2] The surveyor-general was also a crown officer; he had in charge the surveying and bounding of all lands for which warrants were issued. At first each province had such an officer, but after 1739 the crown appointed one person as surveyor-

[1] MS. Warrants, Surveys or Certificates of, Records.
[2] C. R. III, 86; State Records I, 8, 120–21; MS. Warrants and Records.

general and auditor for all of the American colonies, and he appointed a deputy surveyor and a deputy auditor for each colony, and these at his own pleasure.[1] This deputy auditor was both a territorial and a fiscal officer, chiefly fiscal; he audited all accounts of the crown's revenues. He was required to send reports not only to the auditor-general but also to the treasury department in England concerning rents, prizes, fines, forfeitures, customs duties and all other forms of the public revenue. The land patents were also recorded in his office.[2] The receiver-general, as was the case with the deputy auditor, was both a territorial and a fiscal officer. He was to receive rents and all other revenues arising from lands, and had the power of collection, even by means of sale and distress. He was appointed by the crown and was required by it to render full accounts of all monies, to the auditor and surveyor-general of the American colonies.[3] During a part of the royal period there was only one receiver-generalship for both the Carolinas. In consequence of this plan there was much complaint concerning its inefficiency, especially in collecting the revenues from lands. To remedy the defects of such an arrangement, a deputy or an assistant was at times appointed by the governor, the council concurring, to aid in their collection.[4] There was also an inspector or commissioner of territorial revenues, appointed by the crown for the pur-

[1] State Records I, 1–3, 34; C. R. IV, 37–38; VI, 731–32; IX, 644.
[2] State Records I, 3, 34; C. R. V, 21, 622–23, 817; VI, 48, 725, 731–32; IX, 644; MS. Warrants.
[3] State Records I, 4–6.
[4] C. R. III, 26–27, 327–29, 436; IV, 15, 39, 45; V, 422–423, 438–39.

pose of exercising general control over all revenues
arising from lands. It was also his duty to supervise
patents, to inspect the books of all the territorial officers, to investigate frauds and to settle disputes
growing out of territorial affairs.[1]

Connected with the territorial office were two courts,
those of claims and of the exchequer. The first, being
constituted by the governor and council, took into consideration all claims growing out of lands; it sat at
certain places and times, most frequently twice a year,
made investigations, and disposed in some manner
of all the cases presented to it.[2] The court of the exchequer administered justice in all cases arising from
the revenues, the larger part of which came from lands.
This court was erected by the governor and council,
while its presiding officer, the chief baron, was appointed by the crown. Such an official was appointed
in 1732, but there is no record of a court being organized prior to 1735. In addition to the chief baron,
there were assistant barons, an usher and a clerk, all
being appointed by the governor with the concurrence
of the council. As to the actual workings of such a
court we cannot speak with much certainty, as it has
left few records of proceedings. Even as late as 1767
it appears that it had never been recognized; it had
been organized at several times, but had done little or
no business.[3]

[1] State Records I, 1–3, 34–41, 61–65.

[2] C. R. III, 401, 427; IV, 40, 53, 653, 656, 768–70; VII, 442; VIII,
160–61, 193.

[3] C. R. III, 100, 424, 496–98; IV, 37, 38, 44, 208, 276–77; V,
1119–20; VII, 498–99.

Under the crown, as under the patentees, the policy
of issuing fairly small grants was adhered to. There
were, as we have seen, a few large grants made by the
proprietors, but these were unsettled. The crown now
proposed to break these up, or at least instructions
were sent to this effect. The patents called for less
than six hundred and forty acres, though occasionally
they contained as many as one thousand acres, only
once being as large as two thousand.[1] There were a
few exceptions to this policy of issuing fairly small
grants, and these were not made by the provincial land
office, but by the crown's specific orders. In 1737 the
king, advising with the council, issued an order to the
provincial office and the surveyor-general to the effect
that two patents be granted to Henry McCulloh,[2] a London merchant. One containing seventy-two thousand
acres was located on the northeast branch of the
Cape Fear River; the other containing sixty thousand
acres was located at the head of the Neuse River and
upon the upper branch of the Cape Fear. These grants
were made for speculative purposes, not for settlement, at least to any great extent. And during the
same year the king ordered that patents issue to other
London merchants for one million and two hundred
thousand acres on the upper waters of the Pee Dee,
Cape Fear and Neuse rivers, in twelve tracts. These
were likewise mainly for speculative purposes. In

[1] C. R. III, 101–02; MS. Warrants, Surveys, Records.
[2] He had been appointed commissioner for inspecting and controlling
the royal revenues and grants of land in the Carolinas. State Records
I, 31–41.

1745 Governor Johnston, acting upon the orders from the crown, issued at least forty patents, of twelve thousand five hundred acres each, to the associates and assignees of these merchants, also a large number of grants of the same size to Henry McCulloh and his associates.[1] Few, if any, of these patents were properly settled, and being granted mainly for speculative purposes they cannot properly be regarded as constituting an exception to the regular policy of issuing small grants.

The grantee under the crown was in practically the same situation as he had been under the patentees.   He obtained his lands by making a small purchase payment and by pledging himself to pay an annual quit-rent, holding his grant in free and common socage, subject to the obligation of yearly rents and fealty to the crown. The quit-rents, as established under the crown, were as a rule at the rate of four shillings proclamation money per one hundred acres.[2]   These quit-rents were a matter of great importance, both to the crown and the colonists.   As they constituted the chief source of the crown's revenue in the province, and especially the source of the salaries of its officers, the executive looked the more carefully to the maintenance of a high rate. Their rate, the form in which they should be payable, and the places at which payment should be made, became the subject of much dispute and conflict between the executive and the lower house of the legislature during the first ten years of the royal administration.

[1] C. R. IV, 253–54; V, 770–82; VI, 773–74, 996–98; MS. Records.
[2] C. R. III, 102; IV, 54; MS. Warrants.

Since these conflicts, from the point of view of constitutional law, have been discussed in another connection,
here they will be considered solely with reference to
their historical development.

Under the system of quit-rents, as it originated with
the proprietors, the revenue from lands accrued in small
amounts and very slowly, but the rent was payable
forever. As we have seen, the original plan of granting lands subject to quit-rents only was changed to that
of granting for purchase money and quit-rents some
time before the patentees surrendered their claims.
With the introduction of this change it seems that the
rents were less efficiently collected. The colonists were
glad to escape their payment, and the proprietors had
no adequate system of collecting them; the rent-roll was
never completed and there was as yet no law in force
declaring lands vacated unless the quit-rents were properly paid.[1]

This was the condition of affairs when the first royal
governor arrived in 1731. He came with instructions
to issue no grants at a lower rate of quit-rent than four
shillings per one hundred acres, while the colonists had
received most of their lands at one-half this rate, or
less. As a matter of course, they demanded that he
continue to act according to the old and long established
rule, even though contrary to his specific instructions.
The crown would not yield to such demands, and consequently a struggle between the executive and the
lower house went on for the first nine years of the royal

[1] C. R. III, 144, 148, 149.

administration.[1]   The collection of rents during these years was very inefficient.   In 1739, however, an act was passed with the specific object of securing a rent-roll, so that rents might be collected more efficiently. This was the first act of the kind in the history of the province.   In 1747 this act was repealed, exactly why we do not know; it was passed again in 1748, with some modifications particularly in regard to what rents should be payable in and at what rates.[2]   The act of 1748, together with several other territorial acts covering the years from 1715 to 1750, was during 1754 repealed by the crown.   From this time to the end of the royal administration the governor received instructions concerning quit-rents, especially in what they were payable and at what rates commodities might be accepted. He was also to secure a new act concerning quit-rents, the provisions of which would protect the interests of the crown.   Such an act was passed in 1755, with a clause suspending its execution until the crown gave its approval.   This act was found to be as objectionable to the crown as the former ones had been, and apparently the royal approval was never given.[3]   Both parties, the colonists and the crown, were thus opposed to each other; the king was desirous of obtaining the maximum of revenue from the quit-rents, while the colonists were disposed to reduce this in one way or another to a minimum.

[1] C. R. III, 102, 139, 144, 148, 149, 292–93, 337, 632; IV, 287, 425–27; V, 100.

[2] C. R. IV, 416, 846; V, 101–08, 1106; Swann, 85, 275–78, 329.

[3] C. R. V, 448–49; IX, 824, 1007, 1257; Davis,1765, II, 35.

The processioning of lands became a matter of considerable importance. Surveying was very inefficiently done, and disputes concerning boundaries were, therefore, most frequent. But this was a matter for the legislature, only indirectly for the crown. An act was passed in 1723 by the assembly under the patentees, requiring that all lands be processioned every three years and establishing the method by which this should be done. This being amended in 1729, making the penalty for neglect the more severe, was continued in force down at least to 1757, and perhaps to 1773.[1]

Of more importance than processioning was registration. Original patents were recorded in the land office, but transfers and leases most frequently were not so recorded. The patentees had given instructions requiring this, but these were by no means fully obeyed. What system they had prior to 1715, we do not know. The first act pertaining to this subject, of which there is now any record, was passed by the assembly in 1715–1716, though this was perhaps a restatement of an older act. It provided for the appointment of registers in each precinct and defined their powers and duties. This act, as well as the proprietors' instructions, laid down the principle that the first deed, and also the first mortgage, which was registered in the land office was the valid one. Precinct registers were kept until the beginning of the royal period, and most probably to its end, but apparently there was no general registry for the whole province prior to about 1733. Then the auditor, or his deputy, was assigned the duty

[1] Swann, 54, 76; Davis, 1773, 560; C. R. V, 741.

of making a registration for the whole colony,[1] the precinct registers rendering yearly accounts to him.   Such
a plan was intended to secure a greater efficiency of
registration, but it was not properly executed; and the
assembly hindered rather than facilitated its administration.   In 1741 two acts were passed, one extending
the time in which registration could be made, the other
relieving those who had failed to comply with the pro-
visions.of the act of 1715–1716.   Again in 1755, 1756,
1760, 1764, 1766, 1770 and 1773 other acts of relief were
passed.   The records indicate that only one of these
—the act of 1755—was repealed by the crown.   In
registration, as in processioning, the assembly exercised
the chief control.[2]

Next to quit-rents, escheats and forfeitures were most
important.   To both the patentees and the crown they
brought in some revenue.   Their regulation was for the
most part in the hands of the proprietors and the crown,
and was not so fully intrusted to the legislature, as was
the case with processioning and registration.   The system of escheats was much more fully established by an
act of 1715–1716 than it had previously been, and the
conditions were now in part defined.   By the king
lands were granted upon the condition that three acres
out of every fifty should be cultivated within three
years of the issue of the grant; otherwise they escheated
back to the crown.   Not only did the crown define the
terms, but it also appointed an escheator to look after

[1] C. R. I, 79; III, 88; IV, 54; Swann, 19–20.

[2] C. R. VI, 7–8; Swann, 155, 215–76; Davis, 1765, II, 71–72, 83–84,
211–12, 332; Davis, 1773, 344–45, 464, 562.

them. Lands also escheated upon the death of the holder without heirs, and they were forfeited for felony or treason. Granville, as well as the crown, had such a system, the only difference being in the conditions,[1] and these were not important.

Concerning the efficiency of the territorial system and its administration not very much can be said, except to its discredit. Under the patentees there was much looseness, and a good many abuses prevailed. These continued, though not to so great an extent, under the crown. From 1724 to 1729 there is much evidence also of fraudulent grants, and from 1729 until the first royal governor arrived in 1731 a large number of blank patents were issued from the land office—though upon no specific authority from England—which allowed the holders to fill out the number of acres. These, of course, led to much abuse and fraud;[2] they were not recorded when issued from the land office, and they, as well as many regular patents, were not properly registered when transferred. As we have already seen, the assembly passed many acts relieving holders from the penalties of not registering. Under such conditions it was impossible to have anything like a complete rent-roll, and without this quit-rents could not be properly collected. Moreover, the crown officers in control of the territorial administration were at times not very active or intelligent in discharging their duties.

[1] C. R. I, 59–67, 453; II, 305, 317, 323, 451, 452; III, 101, 148, 295; IV, 208; V, 1105, 1135; Swann, 11–12, 90; Granville MS. Warrants and Surveys.

[2] C. R. IV, 417–18; V, 93–97, 587; VI, 600–05, 1073–76; VII, 513–14.

[3] C. R. IV, 417–18; V, 93–97, 587; VI, 600–05, 1073–76; VII, 513–14, 883–84; VIII, 164, 167–68, 196; IX, 260, 602–04, 647–50, 608–10, 653–55.

CHAPTER VI.

THE FISCAL SYSTEM AND ADMINISTRATION.

THE territorial administration, as has been seen, is in any country of very great importance. Connected with it, and of perhaps equally great significance, is the fiscal system, its policy and management. In the province of North Carolina money in some form was necessary, for paying the expenses of the administration and the defence, for discharging the dues of the colonists to the patentees and the crown, and for carrying on commercial transactions. The sources of the public revenue, the form which it assumed, and especially its collection and distribution, were matters of great importance.[1] It was necessary that the provincial government should provide for the public revenues. It was also necessary that it should regulate and control the medium of exchange between colonists and colonists and between them and itself, for upon this depended in a large measure the prosperity of both the government and the colonists.

On all these questions the crown naturally took the point of view of an old and highly developed country, a conservative one, while the colonists upon the whole adopted the notions of pioneer communities, less sound

[1] See Bullock, The Monetary History of the United States, for an excellent statement.

125

and more radical; pioneers in a new and undeveloped
country almost invariably do this. Even among the
colonists themselves there were different views, the
more wealthy as a rule being to a large extent in sympathy with the ideas of economics and finance in general vogue in England, while the poorer ones frequently
favored an unsound and fluctuating monetary system.

What then was the position of the crown, what was
its fiscal policy? Finances being of such great importance, the crown theoretically did not leave much to the
discretion of the provincial officers. The governor was
in this particular placed under many limitations and
restraints, which were intended largely to prevent his
yielding to the demands of the lower house of the legislature. He was especially instructed not to assent to
acts of the assembly which provided for the issue of
bills of credit unless they contained provisions to the
effect that they should not go into operation until the
crown officials in England had passed on them. Many
bills of credit had been issued under the proprietors,
and many abuses had come from them, causing trouble
in commercial transactions. By these instructions
being made so prominent, it would appear that the
crown purposed to regulate the medium of exchange,
rather minutely perhaps. Not only this, but the governor was also to keep the officials in England well informed upon all monetary conditions. And, too, the
auditing of all fiscal accounts was to be done by an
officer of the crown who did not reside exclusively in
one province, the auditor-general of America; and this
officer, as well as the governor, must report at least

twice a year to the treasury department in England and the board of plantations, concerning the public revenues. It is quite clear that the crown intended that, through the provincial executive, it should control these and their expenditures. Though the governor might on occasions allow the assembly to examine into all the accounts of the public moneys, still he was not legally compelled to do this. To be sure this was in actual practice done most frequently, but it was so done in order to secure the friendly feeling of the representatives of the colonists. Not only were the governor and council to control all public revenues, but they were also to regulate the salaries and fees of the public officers, securing, if possible, a confirmation from the assembly.[1]

Such were the purposes of the crown, but owing to the force of circumstances it failed to attain them. It had to yield to many of the desires and demands of the lower house, though contrary to the policy which has been outlined above. However, for the first seventeen years it allowed no issue of bills of credit, with two exceptions, these being for emergencies. In 1748, after many solicitations from the colonists and the lower house, the governor assented to the issue of more of this form of paper money, though it was contrary to his instructions and though there was at the time no great necessity for such action.[2] Six years later the actual state of war compelled another issue, and others still in 1760 and 1761. The crown now determined to

[1] C. R. III, 95–103, 497; V, 1106, 1114; VII, 137–38; VIII, 512.
[2] C. R. VI, 1308; Swann, 266–70.

put an end to the violation of its instructions, the ignoring of its policy, and the evil effects of such large issues of provincial paper, by securing from parliament, during 1764, an act forbidding any American colony to issue further bills of credit, and in 1773 a similar enactment in regard to treasury notes. Debenture notes, however, were allowed to be issued in great emergencies, as in 1768-1769 and 1771.[1]

Though by no means wholly successful in carrying out its policy concerning the issue of paper money, nevertheless the crown was more successful here than it was in its attempts to control the auditing and the disposition of the public revenues. To be sure, the auditor of the crown did examine the accounts of moneys obtained from lands, customs and other sources of the royal revenue, but the two houses of the legislature in practice audited all the accounts of moneys raised or appropriated by the assembly, and these constituted, especially in time of war, the larger part of the public revenues. Though the governor must render accounts of the moneys raised by the assembly, for ordinary or extraordinary purposes, to the home authorities, still for the most part he did not exercise any great control over these. Not only did the legislature in reality audit them; it also appointed the treasurers and commissioners who collected them, and, therefore, had a controlling influence over them. Over the point, as to which body, the executive or the legislature, should regulate and control the public moneys,

---

[1] C. R. VII, 887-88, 915-17; VIII, 5, 6, 9; IX, 76; 4 Geo. III, c. 34; 13 Geo. III, c. 57.

there was a struggle throughout the royal period. This has been under discussion in another connection. Here it is only necessary to state that, as a result of this long conflict, the crown failed in the main to carry its point. And, moreover, the crown failed, even signally, in its attempts to secure from the legislature permanent salaries for the provincial officers, especially the executive; the assembly did not often make such provision even for a year, to say nothing of such a permanent provision.

Prior to 1712 there was apparently no paper currency in the province, and during this period there was very little coin or sterling, the chief form of exchange among the early colonists being barter or commodities. The prices of these commodities were fixed by provincial laws, and they were higher than the market prices. What the exchange ratio between barter and sterling was during the first years of the colony's life we can not say with much certainty, though in 1709 it was three to one;[1] and this was perhaps the lowest during the whole period under the patentees. It now became so low that the proprietors issued an order to their receiver-general to the effect that no more barter should be received in payment of the quit-rents. As the evidence seems to indicate, such an order was not based upon an intelligent understanding of the situation. There was not sufficient gold and silver to pay these rents; the council acted with much more intelligence when in 1713 it ordered that barter should be accepted in payment of the rents, if in good

[1] C. R. I, 715.

9

commodities and at fair market rates. Such an order
on the part of the provincial council was confirmed by
the patentees, and in 1715–1716 they allowed, by accepting an act of the assembly, seventeen different commodities to become legal tender in the payment of all
kinds of debts, the number being increased later.
These were accepted in payment of both quit-rents and
taxes, even to the middle of the eighteenth century,
though many of them did not long pass in the markets
at the rates fixed by the laws.[1]

This barter currency was very inconvenient and at
the same time lacked flexibility; its defects were quite
apparent even in the most backward parts of the province. That the colonists should ask for a change, for
a medium of exchange which was much more easy and
flexible, was, therefore, most natural. Coin they did not
possess to any extent, barter was inconvenient, and a
demand for paper money came; and apparently this demand came rather early in the history of the province.
So far as the records show, the patentees did not make
concession to such demands until in 1712, and then
under the pressure of circumstances. The colony was
now burdened in its efforts to meet the heavy expenses
of carrying on a war with the Tuscaroras, and for the
first time did it feel the need for extraordinary revenue. A tax was levied with which to pay these expenses. To collect it required some time, and, in order
to secure the money at once, 4,000 pounds in bills of
credit were issued. These bills, being interest bearing
for a time, were made legal tender and thus forced

[1] C. R. II, 33–34; III, 185, 615; IV, 292–94, 415, 919–23.

upon the colonists.   By the act of their issue they were
given a value in exchange equal to the barter currency,
sometimes called "proclamation money." The fact
that they were supposed to be paid and taken up in a
comparatively short time caused them to pass at par
for a time. Had the tax been collected, which was not
done rapidly or regularly, and had the legislature not
forced the patentees to accept them in payment of quit-
rents, such an issue would have been fair. But to
force the proprietors, living in England, to accept them
for territorial dues, when they were worth practically
nothing outside of the province, was an act of injustice,
and to delay in collecting the tax, which was to refund
them, was also unfair to the colonists who held them.[1]

When the precedent of issuing bills of credit was once
established, it was not at all easy to resist the demands
on the part of the colonists for a further issue. The
Indian war continued, and the tax for sinking the bills
of the first issue was very slowly collected. These circumstances made it necessary, at least it was so thought
by the lower house, to swell the currency of the province by more paper money; 8,000 pounds more were
emitted during 1713. These bills, like the first, were
made legal tender, and were to be redeemed by a tax
on land and polls. Again the proprietors especially
suffered, as they were forced to accept this paper in
payment of the quit-rents, though it very quickly depreciated. The depreciation was at least 40 per cent.
within the province, and outside of it the paper was
practically worthless. To be sure, the proprietors op-

[1] C. R. I, 838; III, 145, 484–85, 615; IV, 576.

posed such a fiscal policy, but the circumstances were such as to force them to yield.[1]

This, however, was by no means the end of the paper money policy of the legislature. Again in 1714–1715, when the Indian wars were over, it issued 24,000 pounds of bills of credit, in spite of the wishes of the patentees to the contrary. In fact the assembly was now largely in control of the administration, and consequently its fiscal policy was to be extended. This third issue of bills was to sink those of the former emissions—still amounting to almost the original sum, 12,000 pounds—and to pay off the outstanding indebtedness. This affords very strong proof of the fact that practically none of the taxes laid for sinking the first issues had been collected. It is also a remarkable commentary upon the efficiency of the fiscal system. These bills of 1715, bearing no interest, were not limited as to the time in which they were to be redeemed, though a tax was laid upon land and polls for the purpose of sinking them. They were made equal in exchange value to the barter currency, which was now by law at the ratio of 1.5 to 1 sterling. Though made legal tender, still this was not sufficient to cause them to pass at anything like their par value. The legislature anticipated this, and even went so far as to place a considerable penalty upon any member of either house who should speak in any manner whatever derogatory to the public credit. It also enacted that a refusal to accept the bills would be punished by a forfeiture of twice the amount presented and refused.[2] This plan of maintaining the

[1] C. R. II, 50; III, 145, 485; IV, 576.
[2] C. R. III, 177–79, 187, 189, 485; IV, 576.

bills at par was so unnatural and based upon such faulty economic principles that it amounted to nothing, except to show the real situation of the currency. The first two issues had been practical failures, and the assembly proposed to maintain, if possible, by means of arbitrary regulations a system which could not survive upon its own merits. In reality the public credit was not improved or strengthened by such enactments. Within two years of their issue the bills were passing at a very considerable discount, and by 1721 they were on the market at 2.5 to 1 sterling, while by the act of their issue they were given the ratio of 1.5 to 1 sterling; and this depreciation took place in spite of the fact that some of them were being redeemed. Now the proprietors, to protect themselves, were forced to refuse to accept them in payment for lands, either purchase money or quit-rents, though they were accepting "proclamation money," that is barter.[1]

These bills, as we have seen, were to be redeemed by a tax on polls and land. This was very slowly collected, and in 1720 the assembly reduced its rate, in spite of the provision in the act of 1714–1715 to the effect that the said tax should not be reduced until all the bills had been redeemed. By 1722 there were still outstanding of these at least 12,000 pounds—one half of the issue—and to exchange these this amount of new bills was emitted. Though the act of 1722 did not enlarge the paper currency, still the rate of exchange did not improve, bills passing during the years from 1722 to 1729 at about 5 to 1 sterling, a great depreciation.

[1] C. R. II, 250, 270, 417; IV, 576.

Whether or not there was any provision for the sinking of these new bills we cannot say with absolute certainty. Governor Johnston claimed that none was made, while Governor Burrington declared that some provision was made, though a very poor one, and he was most probably correct. Whatever it was, it amounted to little. By 1729 at least 10,000 pounds of these bills were still outstanding, less than 2,000 pounds having been redeemed in seven years.[1]

This was not yet the end of the issue of paper money, though it was passing at a very great discount. In 1729, before the crown assumed control, though after the purchase had been made, 40,000 pounds were issued, in the shape of bills of credit. Of these 10,000 pounds were for the purpose of taking up the old bills, though outstanding bills still existed perhaps to the amount of 12,000 pounds. This would increase the paper currency by about 30,000 pounds, and this amount was to be loaned at six per cent. interest for a term of fifteen years, upon what was supposed to be good security. The interest, together with one fifteenth of the principal, should be paid yearly, thereby sinking the whole issue of 40,000 pounds by the end of this period and leaving a balance to the province of 5,000 pounds. Had the greatest care been taken in loaning this, and especially in accepting the securities, the province might perhaps have been able to redeem the whole issue within fifteen years without laying a tax. Such care was not taken, and the expectations of the assembly were not realized. Many bad securities were accepted

[1] C. R. III, 145, 189–90, 485–86; IV, 178, 576; Swann, 48.

and consequently the loans based upon them failed; and those that were well placed failed to bring in sufficient revenue with which to redeem the bills as provided for in the act of issue. This, as well as the former policy of the assembly in regard to maintaining the currency, caused a considerable depreciation. By 1731 the bills were passing in the province at from 7 or 8 to 1 sterling, while the ratio established by law was 5.17 to 1 sterling.[1]

Such was the fiscal condition of the province when Governor Burrington, the first royal governor, arrived. The colonists demanded that all fees and quit-rents be paid in these depreciated bills, while he was specifically instructed against accepting them. This meant that the crown proposed to change the fiscal conditions and policies which had existed during the last years of the proprietory administration. Such instructions were, however, by no means easily carried out. The colonists, whenever their paper money was refused, did not pay their quit-rents or fees. Moreover, the banking scheme of 1729 failed, at least to a very large extent. By 1735 not one tenth of the money due from the interest and principal of the loans had been paid, and in order to meet current expenses, and supply a better medium whereby the quit-rents, then greatly in arrears, could be paid, the assembly passed an act which provided for a new issue of bills of credit. Governor Johnston was by force of necessity compelled to accept such a plan, though contrary to his instructions from the crown. This act provided for the emission of 40,-

[1] Swann, 71; C. R. III, 145–46, 190; IV, 101–02, 178–79, 419, 576.

000 pounds of paper currency, and it was stated in the act that this amount was for the purpose of exchanging the bills of 1729. This meant that none of the issue of 1729 had been redeemed, that thus again the assembly had broken faith with the public, and that the old bills now greatly depreciated were declared equal in value to the new ones. It was also provided that all moneys accruing from the loans of 1729 should be re-loaned at six per cent. interest, the principal being payable by 1744, at which time the bills of 1729 according to the terms of the act of issue were to be redeemed in full. By the former issues of paper money it had been provided that it should be redeemed as rapidly as possible; but now the paper currency was to be kept at 40,000 pounds for at least ten years,[1] without any redemption during this period.

Nor was this the end of the efforts of the assembly to defeat the wishes of the crown. During the same session of 1735 it also passed an act, to which the governor gave his assent upon the grounds that it was an emergency measure, to the effect that 10,000 pounds of new bills should be issued. For the purpose of discharging some very pressing claims about 14,150 pounds were granted by the assembly to the crown. To obtain this amount a poll tax and a duty upon liquors were levied, to be collected for a term of five years. This, of course, was a slow process, and in order to facilitate the transaction this amount, or at least 10,000 pounds, should be obtained by issuing bills

[1] Swann, 79; C. R. III, 95, 540-41; IV, 78, 164, 169, 179-80, 251, 419, 576-77.

of credit, these to be redeemed within five years by the said tax and duty. So that the assembly had almost at one time emitted 50,000 pounds of paper currency. Nor was this all. It allowed the commissioners, who were appointed for the purpose of issuing the 40,000 pounds for exchanging the outstanding bills, to emit 2,500 pounds more with which to pay their own expenses. Thus in 1735 the province had 52,500 pounds of paper currency, while, if the provisions of the act of 1729 had been carried out, not more than two-thirds of this amount would have been outstanding. With such a large amount of paper currency in circulation, with poor provisions for its redemption, as well as with a record for bad faith on the part of the legislature, these bills of credit rapidly depreciated until they passed at 10 to 1 sterling.[1]

By 1744 all of these bills should have been redeemed, according to the provisions of the acts of issue, but it was upon investigation found that none of them had been taken up. Whether the tax and duty had not been collected, whether they had been collected and used for other purposes than that for which they were specifically assigned, we can not say with certainty. In any case it is clear that the banking scheme of 1729 had failed and that whatever funds had been obtained from the said tax and duty had been used for other than their assigned purposes. Whose fault this was it is impossible definitely to say, though it is most probable that it should be shared by the assembly and the

[1] Swann, 79, 83; C. R. III, 541, 548–49; IV, 175–85, 205, 398–99, 415–16, 419, 421, 552–53, 557–58, 577.

fiscal officers of the province. With such a policy as this, with such continued and consistent breaking of the public faith on the part of the body which issued this currency, it would, of course, greatly depreciate. The 52,500 pounds of bills of credit were now, at the most liberal estimate, worth only 5,000 pounds sterling. The lower house proposed to remedy the extreme fiscal situation by issuing more bills of credit and by virtual repudiation. The new bills were to be valued at the same rate as barter money, 1.5 to 1 sterling. At this rate it would require only about 8,000 pounds of new paper to take up the whole amount of outstanding bills, which was 52,500 pounds. To such a proposition the upper house would not agree, though repudiation was not objected to on principle. Consequently nothing of importance was done toward relieving the situation. It is true that, during the next year, at the request of Governor Johnston, a poll tax was levied for a term of eight years for the purpose of redeeming in part, at least, the outstanding bills. It required much more than this to bring back the paper currency to anything like its par value.[1]

From 1745 to 1748 many requests on the part of the colonists and the members of the lower house were made for a further issue of bills of credit. There was need of money for defence along the coast, also for paying the quit-rents and the salaries, both of which were by 1748 largely in arrears. These conditions made the governor the more ready to yield to the demands for a fur-

[1] Swann, 187; MS. Laws; C. R. IV, 552–53, 557–58, 714–17, 719–32, 734, 738–39, 746–47, 772–73, 779, 782, 788, 791–93.

ther resort to paper money, and accordingly a new issue was allowed, of 21,350 pounds, the whole amount being granted to the crown.   Of this, 6,000 pounds were set aside for coast defence. The remainder was to go toward paying the salaries of the members of the two houses and other officers, and for redeeming the outstanding bills. The act for the issue of these bills established the rate of their exchange, declaring them proclamation money, known from this time as "new proclamation," and making one pound of these equal to seven and one half pounds of the old bills. At such an exchange rate the 52,500 pounds of outstanding paper currency would be equal to 7,000 pounds of the new bills. The new bills were made legal tender in the ratio of 4 to 3 sterling, and were to be redeemed by a poll tax, to be collected as long as any of the bills remained outstanding. Not only was this an act of repudiation, and upon a fairly large scale, but also by it the principle of redeeming bills at any indefinite time, and most probably never, was clearly announced. While this currency did not depreciate so rapidly, as had been the case in several of the earlier issues, still it passed at less than its established rate, and this in spite of the fact of the disappearance of the old barter currency and of a very considerable increase in the population of the province.[1]

For six years there was no further increase in the paper currency. When the French and Indian wars came, and with them a much greater demand for money, bills of credit were again resorted to. The province

[1] Swann, 266–70; C. R. IV, 755, 792–93, 866, 900, 915, 919–23, 1073.

must be defended; forts must be built and equipped, soldiers provisioned and paid. Under these pressing conditions President Rowan, in 1754, gave his assent to a bill granting 40,000 pounds to the crown in the shape of bills of credit. Of this amount, 17,000 pounds were set apart for the purposes of war, while the rest should go toward the paying of debts, the building of school houses, and for contingencies. They were given the same rate of exchange as the issue of 1748, 4 to 3 sterling, and were forced upon the public by being made legal tender. For their redemption a poll tax and a duty upon imported liquors were laid. Still they met with much the same experience as the former issues; they depreciated to a considerable degree within the province, and outside of it they were practically worthless. So great were the inconveniences of such a monetary system that the London merchants trading with the province petitioned the crown in 1759 to take away the legal tender quality of the bills. The crown sent out instructions to the effect that, when these bills were offered to the English merchants, they should be accepted at the option of the merchant and at their exchange ratio on the London market, which was very low indeed.[1]

As the war continued, more and more money was needed; and Governor Dobbs, though desirous of adhering to his instructions from the crown which forbade any further issue of bills of credit, still was moved by force of circumstances to yield to an extent. He gave

[1] Davis, 1765, II, 18–25; C. R. V, 108–09, 440; VI, 16–17, 24–25, 43–45.

his assent to an act for the emission of 3,400 pounds, not in bills of credit, but in treasury notes, to be used for military purposes. These notes were in several respects different from the bills of credit which the assembly had long been in the custom of issuing. They were interest bearing and were to be redeemed at the end of one year, a poll tax and a duty upon liquors being laid for this purpose. Nor was this the only issue of these treasury notes, as during 1757 and 1758 there were issued of this kind of currency, and under the same general conditions, 25,806 pounds, making, with the earlier issue, 29,206 pounds. It is worthy of special remark that the assembly and fiscal officers of the province now kept faith with the public in a far more honorable way than they had done in the case of the bills of credit. By 1764 interest had been paid on these notes to the amount of 1,370 pounds, while by the same time 23,807 pounds, principal and interest, had been redeemed.[1] While these treasury notes brought relief to the province, still they did not by any means restore it to a good fiscal condition. The bills of credit of 1748 and 1754 were not being redeemed at all rapidly, and were consequently depreciating. Though the population was rapidly increasing and, therefore, causing a greater demand for money, by 1759 they were passing at 1.9 to 1 sterling. In 1760 Governor Dobbs asked for a modification in the conditions, even though it were necessary to emit more bills of credit. An act was passed during this year for the issue of 12,000 pounds more of this kind of legal tender paper money. Again the assembly placed no limit to the time within

[1]Davis, 1765, II, 80; C. R. VI, 1309–10.

which the bills should be redeemed, though it made a general provision for their redemption by levying a poll tax. This issue was followed during the next year by another of 20,000 pounds, and with the same general provisions. Both of these acts, though contrary to the royal instructions, were assented to by Governor Dobbs, largely from military necessity.[1]

By the issues of such bills in 1748, 1754, 1760 and 1761, 93,350 pounds had been put into circulation. By 1764 there had been redeemed of this amount 25,286 pounds, leaving outstanding 68,064 pounds. There was also still unredeemed the sum of 6,769 pounds in treasury notes, making the paper currency then in circulation, 74,833 pounds. This was apparently not too large a currency, as the population was at least 200,000. This was, however, not all of the money then in circulation. Much barter was still used in the western counties, while inspector's notes were in circulation in the eastern portions of the province.[2]

Though in 1764 an act was passed by the parliament against any further issues of bills of credit by any American province, still this did not put an end to the desire of the colonists of North Carolina for more inflated paper currency. It did, however, stop the issue of the special form of currency known as bills of credit and that in spite of many entreaties on the part of the lower house and the colonists, especially of those living in the western frontier counties, where there was prac-

[1] Davis, 1765, II, 189–92, 220–23; C. R. VI, 17.
[2] C. R. VI, 1046–47, 1308–11; VII, 145, 289, 539; preface, pp. xviii–xix.

tically no coin and where their commodities were not legal tender in payment of taxes and debts.[1]

Though no further issues of these bills were allowed and though the 74,833 pounds in circulation in 1764, and afterwards, was apparently not too large an amount of currency, still the bills did not maintain their par value. By 1767 they were passing at 1.82 to 1 sterling while by the acts of issue their ratio was made 1.33 to 1. They were also being redeemed much more rapidly than had hitherto been the custom. By 1768 at least 15,000 pounds had been taken up; and this most probably would have improved the public credit had the assembly, during 1768, not resolved to discontinue the taxes levied for the redemption of the bills of 1760 and 1761, though in reality they had not had their full effect.[2] Not only did the assembly now propose to take away some of the sources of revenue whereby its public promises could be redeemed, but it also issued more paper currency, though not of the type of bills of credit. The lower house was very strong in its demands that 30,000 pounds of bills be emitted, notwithstanding the act of parliament to the contrary; a compromise was reached between it and the executive to the effect that 20,000 pounds of debenture notes be issued. The assent of Governor Tryon to the act was partly due to the fact that there was an outstanding debt of 4,844 pounds, incurred during the first campaign against the "regulators," and to the other fact that he was very desirous of finishing his fifteen thousand dollar palace at Newbern. Though the assembly

[1] C. R. VII, 497, 619–21, 678–79, 866–67; VIII, 16–18, 75–84.
[2] C. R. VII, 491, 493, 983; VIII, 10, 12, 215.

again swelled the paper currency, already depreciated, still it did not force these notes upon the public by making them legal tender. They were also to be redeemed by a tax levied on polls. According to Governor Martin's account these notes did not, however, relieve the fiscal situation to any considerable extent.[1]

Again, during 1771, the assembly entreated the crown to allow another issue of bills of credit, for the purpose of meeting the expense of about 40,000 pounds, which had been incurred in the second expedition against the "regulators." Again its requests were refused. The crown was now determined to live up to the principles of the act of parliament of 1764. In December of this year, upon an investigation being made, it was found, according to Governor Martin's report, that 42,800 pounds of the bills of credit were still unredeemed and that there was an indebtedness of another kind of about 60,000 pounds. Martin, realizing the very bad state of the fiscal system, asked the crown to allow a further issue of bills, with which to take up the old ones and with which to discharge the floating debts. The permission was given upon the condition that the new issues were not made legal tender. The lower house, however, was not satisfied with this; it demanded that 120,000 pounds of debenture notes be emitted, a sum considerably larger than was absolutely needed, and that these be forced upon the public by being made legal tender in the payment of all debts except those due to British merchants. Governor Martin would not accept such a bill, though he was willing to compromise

[1] Davis, 1773, 342–43, 394–95; C. R. VII, 887–88, 915–17; VIII, 5, 6, 9; IX, 66–69.

the matter by allowing an act for the issue of 60,000 pounds of such notes, provided they were not given the legal tender value. This compromise proposition was accepted by the lower house. Notes to this amount were emitted, with a provision in the shape of a poll tax for their redemption.[1] This issue of notes increased the paper currency of the province to about 100,000 pounds. There was at this time a population of about 250,000, and for this population the currency was by no means too large in amount. However, it did not pass at par, 1.33 to 1 sterling, but at 1.60 to 1.[2]

Thus, as we have seen, the province obtained the larger part of its revenue from lands, quit-rents and purchase money, from poll and land taxes, from customs duties upon the importation of liquors, and from tonnage duties.[3]

This revenue was collected by the territorial officers and by the sheriffs and collectors of customs. The territorial and customs officers, being largely under the control of the crown, were not the occasion of dispute between the provincial executive and the legislature. The sheriffs, and especially the treasurers, who received, kept and paid out the public moneys, were subjects of much contention between the governor and the lower house. The appointment and control of the treasurer, or treasurers, were of great importance to both parties, and to the efficiency of the whole fiscal administration.

[1] Davis, 1773, 496–97; C. R. VIII, 450, 463, 471, 496; IX, 65, 67–69, 72–75, 134, 221–22, 275, 278.
[2] C. R. IX, preface, p. xv; McRee's Iredell I, 14–15.
[3] Swann, 16, 80, 241–44, 343, 355–59; Davis, 1765, II, 111; MS. Laws.

10

Elsewhere the conflicts which arose from these have been discussed. Here they will be considered solely for the purpose of showing what the policy of the colonists, as manifested through the lower house, was in this particular. As early as 1715 there was a law requiring public treasurers to render to the assembly accounts of all moneys received or disbursed by them, and this was in force as late as 1752, and probably much later. The assembly throughout the royal period passed acts appointing these officers, defining their duties, and prescribing the methods of the collection and disbursement of public funds, whether by sheriffs or treasurers, or by both;[1] and these laws afford abundant evidence to the effect that the assembly exercised practical control in all such matters.

The taxes were of two kinds, direct taxes and customs duties. Between 1713 and 1771 direct taxes were levied at least fourteen times on polls, twice on land, and once on law suits. Customs duties were levied twice on the importation of general merchandise and at least six times on the importation of liquors, wines and rum. A tonnage duty was at several times collected for the purpose of supplying a public magazine of ammuntion.[2]

As taxation was frequently resorted to, and as it was the source of much of the public revenue, one would think that the provincial executive and legislature

[1] Swann, 39, 85, 97, 116, 130, 247–50, 307, 327–29, 341, 363–64; Davis, 1765, II, 60–70, 113, 335–61; Davis, 1773, 342, 405–07, 490, 543, 545; MS. Laws.

[2] C. R. III, 189, 485; IV, 576–77; VI, 1309; Swann, 16, 80, 83, 184, 187, 241–44, 266–70, 342–43, 355–59; Davis, 1765, II, 18–23, 111–17, 189–92, 220–23; Davis, 1773, 426, 490, 496–97; MS. Laws.

would give most serious consideration to the method and machinery of their assessment and collection. Such, however, does not appear to have been the case. As a rule, the securing of the funds was the chief object, little attention being given as to how this should be done. To be sure, the sheriffs and the treasurers, to whom were entrusted the listing of taxables and the collecting of taxes, were in a general way instructed as to their duties and powers, though not at times very specifically. So also were the collectors of the customs duties. In selecting the tax on polls as the chief source of revenue the provincial officers and the legislature were acting upon the ideas of taxation then in general vogue, though not so much upon the correct idea, the ability to pay. To have nothing but a uniform poll tax was very unfair, especially to the poorer classes, and this unfairness was recognized by the assembly. In defining what a taxable was, who should pay a poll tax, it attempted to distribute the burdens of such a system as much as possible upon those who were able to bear them. It acted upon the assumption that the number of slaves owned by any one person was for the most part a fair statement of his wealth; and upon this assumption it passed acts defining a taxable, the act of 1750 being the most complete of these. According to this act a taxable was every white man of sixteen years of age, every negro, mulatto or mustee, and every other person of blood mixed to the fourth generation of twelve years of age. By such a definition of a taxable many of the burdens of a poll tax were placed upon the wealthy class, the slave-holding class.[1]

[1] C. R. III, 187; Swann, 85, 180–82, 320–21; Davis, 1765, II, 202–07.

CHAPTER VII.

The Judicial System and Administration.

The executive and legislative features of the royal administration of North Carolina, in their functions and workings, have been under consideration and discussion. Connected with these there is always the judicial feature. To find out how this phase of the provincial government worked itself out and what were its relations to the crown, the colonial executive and the legislature, is the problem of this chapter. This feature, as well as the legislative aspect of the province's political life, was to a large extent, theoretically at least, under the control of the executive; and all three of these were more or less under the direction of the crown. This threefold system was developed to a considerable extent under the proprietors. It was copied from the old English system, and was kept up with slight changes under the royal administration of the province.

As we have seen, the crown appointed and controlled the chief of the executive and legislative departments —the governor. It also appointed the chief justice and more or less defined his powers and duties, thus placing the whole system of justice under many restraints. Such an officer was to a large extent independent of the governor, though in a general way he

148

was under the supervision of the chief executive.   The subordinate officials in the department of justice were, on the other hand, largely under the direction and control of the executive and the legislature.[1]   What then were the policies of the crown and of the representatives of the colonists toward this feature of government?   What forms did this feature assume?

The head of the system was, in theory, the governor, he being the crown's chief representative in the province.   However, he was largely hedged in by limitations.   He had the general supervision of the administration of justice, acting in accord with his instructions from England.   Not only was he under certain restrictions concerning the workings of the system, but also in regard to what privileges he should grant to the colonists.[2]   With the governor as the general supervisor, the crown gave to the province courts of exchequer, admiralty, chancery, superior pleas and grand sessions, oyer and terminer, inferior pleas and quarter sessions, and of magistrates; and this system which was established by the crown was in many respects like that under the patentees.

The court of exchequer has been considered under the territorial system, being a court for the trial of cases arising from the crown's revenues, which were to a large extent obtained from lands.   As we have seen, this court did practically no business, as the chief

---

[1] C. R. III, 102–04, 496–98; V, 1104, 1123–24; VII, 137–42; VIII, 512–16.

[2] C. R. III, 102–04, 496–98; V, 1104, 1123–24; VII, 137–42; VIII, 512–16.

justice of the province demanded that such cases be passed upon by the general court, over which he was the presiding officer. Prior to 1696 there was no admiralty court in the province and the work of such a nature was done by the general court. The admiralty court was now erected by the crown, even though the patentees made the claim that, by their charters, the powers of erecting it were given to themselves. The governor was made vice admiral, and the admiralty office in England appointed a judge, register, marshal and advocate. Whether this court continued in operation throughout the remaining part of the proprietary period it is impossible to say with accuracy, though probably it did. Its records of proceedings during the proprietary and royal administrations are for the most part lacking. This court was in fact not a provincial institution. It was at no time under the control of the officers of the province, but always under the direction of the board of admiralty of England.[1] On the other hand, the chancery court was exclusively a provincial establishment, and so were all the courts mentioned above excepting the admiralty. It, like the courts of exchequer and admiralty, was the creation of the crown, not of the legislature of the colony. Though not erected by the assembly, still a few acts were passed by it looking toward its regulation. This was one of the oldest of the province's judicial establishments, coming in almost as early as the proprietary government. But it was not in session regularly at many different times. It was composed of the governor and

[1] C. R. I, 471–73, 490, 510; III, 82; IV, 223–24; VII, 459–60, 498.

at least five councillors, having also a clerk and at times a master in high chancery. A court of such a composition was not easy to get together, and consequently it did not meet regularly. To correct this defect Governor Martin, in 1771, made an attempt to secure from the authorities in England a very substantial modification of its composition. He asked that the governor alone, or that the governor assisted by two or three masters in chancery, should hold its sessions. This court was in a general way one of equity, not of law, but as to the exact nature of many of its cases we can not speak with certainty, its meagre records bearing indefinite testimony.[1]   In theory it was also the highest court of appeal; in actual practice this position belonged to the superior court.

At the head of the regular law courts was the chief justice, an officer appointed by the crown's warrant and at the crown's pleasure. His powers and duties were specified in the commission which was issued to him, from the crown, upon his appointment. The legislature for the most part had little influence over him. It did, however, secure the insertion of certain clauses in the acts erecting superior courts, which placed restrictions upon him in the discharge of his duties. It could also make complaints concerning his official conduct, and had the power to try him for misconduct. But upon the whole, the chief justice was independent, not only of the legislature, but also of the executive. This position was one of great dignity and influence

[1] C. R. III, 150; IV, 44; V, 823–24, 1085; VI, 75, 1042; VIII, 37; IX, 280, 299–300; Swann, 6, 225, 228.

and for the most part it was filled by men of intelligence and ability. Among these were: William Smith, John Palin, William Little, Daniel Hamner, John Montgomery, Enoch Hall, Eleazer Allen, Peter Henley, James Hassell, Charles Berry, and Martin Howard.[1] It should be noted that several of these were also councillors, as such having much executive power, and as councillors were also members of the legislature. By such an arrangement the executive, legislative and judicial departments were by no means separate and distinct. This condition brought on much criticism from the more democratic elements and it was one against which the makers of the state constitution, when the province was transformed into a state, made provision. They in their reaction went so far as not only to make these separate in their composition but also to place the executive and judicial departments under the practical control of the legislature.[2]

Connected with the chief justice in the superior court of pleas and grand sessions, afterward called the general or supreme court, was another officer appointed by the crown—the attorney general. He, like the chief justice, being appointed by the king's warrant, held his office at the pleasure of the crown, though his official conduct might be called into account by the governor and council.[3] Both of these officers, being crown

[1] State Records I, 9, 74, 112–13, 132–33, 142–43, 209; C. R. III, 85, 86, 136, 416, 423, 552–57, 629; IV, 466–67, 637; V, 962, 991; VI, 66–67, 581; IX, 1018–20.

[2] C. R. III, 85–86; IV, 470; VII, 137; X, 1007–08.

[3] State Records I, 7–8, 109, 136–37, 144, 212; C. R. III, 239; V, 614; VI, 51, 65–66, 568–69, 1067, 1072–73; VII, 444, 523.

officials, were supposed to receive their salaries out of
the crown's revenues, quit-rents and other territorial
dues, but as these were inefficiently collected, they were
poorly paid. In addition to their salaries from the
crown they were entitled to certain fees which were
established by the assembly; and the legislature at
times granted them special allowances. These were
always made for short terms, their renewal being
wholly at the discretion of the assembly. By such a
provision these officers, who were theoretically responsible to the crown alone, became servants of the
assembly.[1]

What were the composition, powers and workings of
this supreme court over which the chief justice presided? Under the proprietors it was made up of the
chief justice and two or more assistants and had the
powers and duties of the king's bench, the common
pleas and the exchequer courts in England. During
the proprietary period the chief justice was appointed
and commissioned by the patentees, while the assistants
were appointed by the governor and council. The
times and places of the meetings were for the most
part arranged by acts of the assembly. When the
crown assumed control of the province no great modifications were made in this court. Now the chief justice
received his appointment and instructions from the
crown, and he alone could hold the supreme sessions;
his assistants were simple justices of the peace, having

[1] C. R. III, 197–98, 278, 283; IV, 982; V, 16, 20–22; VIII, 814;
Swann, 6, 227, 250–58, 304, 325; Davis, 1765, II, 130, 241; Davis, 1773,
476.

no powers as assistants apart from the chief justice. Prior to 1739 this general court had met at Edenton, but now, by an act of the assembly, provision was made for its meeting at several places, for its becoming a circuit court. Such a provision proved efficient, and in 1746 the principle of this court holding its sessions in circuit was permanently established. By this act of 1746 the whole system of the law courts was remodeled, and especially in its administration. Newbern was made the center, in the place of Edenton which now in consequence of the great growth of the population of the province, especially to the south and west, was in one corner of the province. At Newbern this court must hold at least two annual sessions. The chief justice was to have associated with him three associate justices, and these were to have more power than the old assistants. In his absence they could hold the court, hear and determine the cases presented to it, though all processes issuing from the general court must be signed by the chief justice. These changes not only brought greater efficiency into the judicial administration, but they also gave the assembly more power over it, as they were introduced by it rather than by the crown.[1]

Now all writs and processes should be issued from, and filed in, the office of the general court at Newbern, and so must all pleadings and proceedings, whether of the central court or of those on the circuit. However, a trial could take place at Newbern or at the other places on the circuit during any of the *nisi prius* terms.

[1] C. R. III, 150, 215, 251, 423; IV, 45, 734; V, 569; Swann, 91, 224, 228, 233.

Three places were established by the act for the holding of these sessions of the circuit—Edenton, Halifax and Wilmington. Such a plan of dividing the province into districts and of erecting courts in each greatly facilitated the administration of justice and at the same time relieved the colonists of the burdens of traveling a long distance.[1] This new system and its administration were provided for by an act of the assembly, and so were the associate justices. The fact that the crown allowed this act to go into operation and to continue for several years as the basis of the supreme court is strong evidence that the legislature was more and more gaining control over the judicial system and administration. During 1760, another act was passed by the assembly which provided for general sessions, in the main of the same nature as those of 1746. In the clauses appointing associate justices and defining their qualifications and term of office the assembly was assuming unto itself much more power over the administration of justice than it had hitherto done. This act was disallowed by the crown because of these clauses. By it associate justices were appointed *quamdiu se bene gesserint,* while the chief justice held at the pleasure of the king. Appointments for good behavior, which the act provided for, meant the taking from the crown of the power of control over the associate justices, meant the practical independence of the judiciary of the crown, and that the legislature was to exercise the controlling influence over justice.[2]

[1] Swann, 224–40.

[2] C. R. VI, 280, 587–81; Swann, 324–26; Davis, 1765, II, 188.

Though the act of 1760 was repealed by the crown, the assembly during 1762 passed another act which in many particulars was the same as the acts of 1746 and of 1760; and this was allowed by the crown to go into operation. By it the province was divided into five districts for superior courts of pleas and grand sessions and the method of their procedure was prescribed. This act kept the old fourfold divisions for the eastern part of the province, with Edenton, Halifax, Newbern and Wilmington as the centers, but it went beyond the provisions of the act of 1739. The great growth of the colony westward demanded that a district be made out of this portion, and a western district was erected, with Salisbury as its center. The circuit courts in the four eastern districts were to be held by the chief justice and one associate justice, whom the governor had the power of appointing. But to the Salisbury district, being very extensive in area, covering almost as much territory as the four eastern divisions together, was assigned a special judge of its own. He had the full power of holding the grand sessions in the absence of the chief justice, though he was to act as an assistant judge whenever the chief justice was present. By the act of its erection, this court on the circuit was given the power over all pleas of the crown (treason, felony and other crimes committed in breach of the peace), suits in common pleas, legacies and estates of intestates, whether original or on appeal from the inferior courts by means of a writ of error. This definition of its jurisdiction was by no means new, for such had been the jurisdiction of the supreme court from the first of the royal administration. But by this act the control of the legislature over justice was extended beyond that as provided for in the act of 1746. The provision which allowed the associate justice to hold court in the absence of the chief justice restricted the latter's powers to a very considerable degree. Not only did the assembly restrict the chief justice, but it also placed limits upon the powers of the attorney-general. It likewise prescribed the frequency and duration of the sessions, the manner in which suits should be brought, witnesses and other persons summoned, how deposition should be taken and who could bear testimony.[1]

The system as provided in this act proved to be fairly effective and for the most part satisfactory to all parties. It was reënacted with slight changes two years later, and when this act of 1764 expired a new one was passed, during 1767, with many of the provisions of the acts of 1762 and 1764 in it. By the act of 1767 another district was established, due to an increase of population, with Hillsboro as its center, and two associate justices were appointed in the place of one.[2] Early in 1773, when this act was about to expire, the assembly passed another. It divided the province into six districts for the sessions of the supreme court and defined their jurisdiction and proceedings. This act, while for the most part with the same provisions as the former one, contained two important additions. It provided that no suit should, except on appeal, be brought before

[1] Davis, 1765, II, 238–56.
[2] Davis, 1765, II, 353–54; Davis, 1773, 372–86.

these sessions in cases of debts or damages of smaller amounts than fifty pounds, the plaintiff and defendant residing in the same district, and of twenty-five pounds, the parties residing in different districts. It also made provision for the attachment of the goods of persons living outside of the province. To these two provisions the governor offered a serious protest. But the act containing them passed after a long and bitter conflict and in spite of Governor Martin's opposition. However, it contained a clause to the effect that it should not go into operation until the crown had passed upon it. By the limitations placed upon the supreme court, which was theoretically under the control of the crown, and by the extension of the jurisdiction of the inferior courts, which were largely under the influence of the legislature, the assembly was more and more extending its influence over the administration of justice. By its claims concerning the attachment of the goods of foreigners it was practically declaring itself independent of the crown. It was natural, therefore, that the crown should refuse to allow such an act to go into operation, even though for a short period.[1]

During 1774 Governor Martin rejected a bill erecting superior courts, chiefly because it contained the clauses which have been mentioned above; and the attempt of the next year on the part of the legislature looking to the same object met with no greater success. The province had now for three years been without a supreme court, and the needs for such a court were very press-

[1] Davis, 1773, 511–30; C. R. IX, 442, 446–47, 579, 583, 586–87, 670, 619, 685, 707–08, 814.

ing, but neither party was willing to yield its claims
and demands. As will be seen in another connection,
the conflicts arising from these became very serious,
constituting one of the important causes of the downfall of the royal administration. The legislature had
by degrees assumed more and more control over the
superior courts, which at the beginning were largely
under the direction of the crown, and this had for the
most part been permitted by the crown until 1773.
Now the assembly practically asked that the higher, as
well as the lower courts, be under its control.[1]

Below the supreme court was the court of oyer, terminer and general jail delivery, and this came down
from the proprietary period. It was a criminal court
and was composed of the chief justice, two or more
assistants, members of the council, and the other high
officials of the province. Upon the crown assuming
control of the provincial administration, this court was
continued and the governor was instructed to call at
least two sessions of it yearly. Burrington and Johnston in obedience to their instructions and upon the
advice of the council, issued commissions to the chief
justice, the assistants, and the councillors, authorizing
them to hold such sessions; the chief justice and any
three of the others were to constitute a quorum. In
1746 it was provided, by an act of the assembly, that
the governor should commission the chief justice alone
to hold two yearly sessions of oyer and terminer in the
three districts of the superior court. This act also provided the manner in which trials should be brought and
specified the crimes in the trial of which these sessions

[1] C. R. IX, 862–63, 926–28, 988, 1190–95, 1201–11; MS. Laws.

had jurisdiction, declaring them to be treasons, felonies, and misdemeanors. Such provisions converted the general court on the circuits into a special court of oyer and terminer for the trial of criminals. These special sessions could not be held unless the governor issued special commissions to this effect.[1] Here, as in the case of the general courts, the legislature was extending its influence. The crown at first allowed it, but in 1754 another act was passed concerning these special courts and the crown repealed it, on what grounds we can not say. However, this did not put and end to the attempts on the part of the assembly to control these criminal sessions. During 1756 an act was passed to this effect, the chief provisions of which were in 1762, and again in 1764 and 1767, incorporated into the act erecting the general or superior courts of pleas. According to the act of 1762 the chief justice and one or more associates should hold criminal sessions on the circuit, under the authority of the governor's special commission, when he and the council deemed it necessary. When the act of 1767 erecting general courts expired, during 1773, the provisions for special criminal sessions did also. Inasmuch as no further act for superior courts could be passed, the governor, with the concurrence of the council, issued commissions for such criminal sessions upon his own authority. The chief executive had this power all the time, though the assembly was not inclined to recognize it. But from 1746 to 1773 it appears that he had not exercised it; he had allowed the assembly to make provisions for such

[1] C. R. III, 105, 150, 251, 256, 416; IV, 3, 48, 218, 224; Swann, 225–27.

courts, he in a formal way issuing the commissions.
While he, during 1773, provided for these sessions independently of the assembly, still this was apparently
done as an emergency measure. However, it was
severely criticised and denounced as a usurpation on
the part of the governor. The legislature during the
next year regained its control over these sessions.
Now the court of oyer and terminer was much more
definitely defined, its powers and jurisdiction being
quite specifically stated in the act.[1] Governor Martin
gave his assent to such an act, most probably by virtue
of the necessity of circumstances and to an extent to
conciliate the representatives of the colonists.

In the trial of cases which came before the criminal
sessions of the general court the jury system was in
constant use, both the grand and the petit. It came
down from the proprietary period, being established
by their instructions and by acts of the assembly, after
the old English model. Practically no changes were
made in the system and its regulation, as established
under the patentees, until 1748. Now, by an act, jurors
were provided for in all cases, criminal or civil; the
method of their selection, their duties, privileges and
remuneration, were all provided for. This act meant
much greater efficiency in the administration of the system, and its principles were also incorporated in the
acts of 1760, 1762, 1764, 1767 and 1773.[2]

[1] Davis, 1765, II, 34, 80, 255; MS. Laws; C. R. V, 570, 760; VII,
842–46; VIII, 185, 235–40, 490, 507, 528–32; IX, 607, 641, 673–75,
945–46.
[2] C. R. III, 106, 152, 191; IV, 745; Swann, 263–65; Davis, 1765, II,
34, 269–72, 356–58; Davis, 1773, 388–91, 548–50; MS. Laws.

11

The lower or inferior courts of pleas and quarter sessions were, as in the case of the superior pleas, in operation when the province became royal. Under the patentees, these had been held by the justices of the peace, whom the governor appointed. They were held in several sessions yearly and were for the trial of civil cases where the amount involved was less than fifty pounds. In addition to its purely judicial functions, this precinct court had also the administration of the estates of orphans and the supervision of highways and bridges. The assembly here, as in the case of the superior courts, had much influence. Under the proprietors, at least during the latter part of their administration, it established and regulated the inferior sessions. The system of the patentees was allowed to continue until 1746. Now the whole judicial system and administration were reorganized, the superior as well as the inferior courts. By the act of 1746 the precinct or county courts were much more fully formulated. Four sessions yearly must be held in each county by three justices of the peace, who were appointed by the governor and council. These, when in session, had the power of hearing and deciding all matters in common law wherein the amount in litigation was above forty shillings and not more than twenty pounds, actions of *trespass and ejectment* and *writs of formedon* being excepted. They also could hear petty larcenies, assaults, batteries, trespasses, breaches of the peace, and all other offences of an inferior nature, forgery and perjury being excepted. They were also to hear all cases of legacies, intestate estates and matters concerning orphans. From these courts, provision was made for appeal to the superior court. The prosecuting officer in these county sessions was not the attorney-general, as in the case of the general court or the oyer and terminer sessions, but a deputy appointed for each county by the attorney-general.[1]

In 1754 by an act, the assembly not only defined the powers and duties of the inferior sessions, but also enlarged their jurisdiction. This act was repealed by the crown. That this was done because of the extension of the jurisdiction we can not say with absolute certainty, though most probably it was for this reason. These sessions were almost wholly under the control of the provincial officers, and especially of the legislature, and to extend their jurisdiction meant further limitation of the superior courts, which were to a large extent under the direction of the crown. But the repeal of the act of 1754 was not sufficient to keep the legislature from bringing the matter under further consideration. In 1760 an act was passed which again extended the jurisdiction of the inferior courts, now to cases involving fifty pounds. The crown, on the other hand, was not disposed to yield to such extension of the influence of the colonists, and this act also was repealed. It was, however, in operation for a time, how long we can not say. The assembly now gave up, at least temporarily, its demands on this point and passed, during 1762, an act which limited the jurisdiction of inferior sessions to twenty pounds. However, at the same time it passed another act providing for the trial by these

[1] C. R. I, 574; II, 526, 570; III, 150, 191, 194; Swann, 51–52, 235–39.

sessions of the cases involving as much as fifty pounds, which had been begun but not completed according to the act of 1760. The provisions of the act of 1762 were continued, though with slight modifications, in the acts of 1764 and 1768.[1] During 1773, the question of extending the jurisdiction of the lower courts again came up. After much dispute concerning it between the lower house and the governor, another act was passed providing that the inferior courts should have jurisdiction in cases involving amounts as large as fifty pounds. Governor Martin gave his assent to such an act, being driven to it by force of conditions. The crown repealed it. It was willing to allow the officers of the courts to be appointed by the provincial officials, and that their powers, duties and methods of procedure be defined by the assembly. It was also willing that within small limits these sessions be practically independent of the crown, but it would not allow this independence to be great in its extent.[2]

Below the quarter sessions there was a still smaller court, the court of one or two magistrates, the lowest of all the judicial departments. It had jurisdiction in actions for smaller amounts than those prescribed for the regular inferior sessions. This session of the magistrates was perhaps one of the oldest of the provincial courts. In the laws of 1715–1716 there was one making provision for such sessions, and this was most probably a reënactment of a much older law or custom.

---

[1] Davis, 1765, II, 34, 111, 188, 256–69, 354–56, 386–88; MS. Laws; C. R. V, 298–300; VI, 588–89.

[2] C. R. IX, 583, 587, 619, 670; Davis, 1773, 523–26; MS. Laws.

This court was also provided for by acts of 1729 and 1741. Each precinct or county had several magistrates, appointed by the governor and council, and these by their sessions had much to do in keeping the peace and in administering justice in an elementary way.[1]

For each of these courts, excepting those of the magistrates, there was need of a special officer who should keep the records of the sessions and make reports whenever they were demanded—a clerk. This clerk in addition to being a purely administrative official had some judicial duties. The clerk of the pleas of the crown was the highest of these officers. Prior to 1761–1762 the secretary of the province was also clerk of the pleas of the crown, there being no separate officer for these, at least so far as the records indicate. After 1762 a clerk was appointed by the crown, with a tenure of office depending upon its pleasure. But he appointed the clerks of the county courts during good behavior. It was frequently claimed, and there is some evidence substantiating such a claim, that by appointing clerks for good conduct the clerk of the pleas of the crown obtained a large amount of money in the shape of a bonus. While the clerks of the county courts were appointed by the clerk of the pleas of the crown and were, therefore, more or less amenable to him, still they were under the general direction of the magistrates of the county, being by them placed under a bond for their official conduct. How the clerks of the sessions of the county were appointed before 1762 we can not state with certainty. Perhaps the secretary

[1] Swann, 77, 145–46; C. R. III, 183; III–IX, passim.

did it during a part of the time. The assembly by an
act of 1740 proposed to appoint them, but this act was
repealed by the crown.[1] Who appointed the clerks of
the general court on the circuit prior to 1746 we cannot say, though most probably the chief justice. At
least this was the case after 1746. By the acts of the
assembly of 1746 and 1760 he was authorized to appoint
a clerk for each district of the circuit. These clerks
were under bond to the crown for their official conduct,
just as the clerks of the county courts were to the justices of the peace of the counties. After 1762, when
a separate clerk of the pleas of the crown was appointed, he claimed the right of appointing the clerks
of the superior court on the circuit. This was opposed
to the provisions of the acts of the assembly which
authorized the chief justice to do this, and the matter
was referred to the authorities in England. What decision was rendered we do not know, though it is probable that the provisions of the assembly were allowed.[2]

Such were the different courts and their officers, and
such were their jurisdiction, functions, powers and
duties. What their actual procedure was we can not
state with very much certainty. The records bear
abundant testimony that the whole system was neither
permanent nor very definite. It could be changed
rather easily, and it was, therefore, frequently modified.
As a rule the acts erecting the different courts were for

[1] C. R. VI, 564, 689–90; VII, 114; IX, 264–67, 981, 1004–05; State
Records I, 8, 120–21; Swann, 110.

[2] Swann, 227; Davis, 1765, II, 240; Davis, 1773, 373, 440; C. R. VI,
1001; VIII, 19.

a short period only, thus permitting the administration of justice to become the subject of frequent contention between the different parties, always allowing the possibility of having no courts at all. That the system and administration of justice should under these conditions be rather inefficient and even chaotic at times is not at all strange; it was perfectly natural. But most probably the royal government was in this respect about as successful as it was in all the others. We find a condition of inefficiency, and even chaos, in the executive, legislative and judicial departments, and we find the same condition in the administration of territorial, fiscal and military affairs. This was due in part to the lack of intelligence on the part of the crown, to a lack of intelligence, industry and character on the part of the crown officials in the province, as well as to a lack of intelligence and energy on the part of the representatives of the colonists.

CHAPTER VIII.

The System of Defence.

Every province or state must have some system of defence, some means of military protection against enemies from without, as well as against insurrection and rioting within. North Carolina, whether under the proprietors or crown, had her system, and this was very similar to that of the other English colonies. This, as well as the other departments, had its changes and development, depending much upon the disposition of the Indians and the French. The four intercolonial wars between the English and the French colonists mark distinct periods in the development of the system of defence in almost every one of the provinces. The provincial system was to be used not only for local defence, but also for carrying out in great emergencies the British colonial policy, which was distinctly one of expansion. North Carolina, as well as the other colonies, was called upon for aid to such a policy.

With some modifications the following system was more or less in operation, and it was theoretically in force throughout the colonial period. As we have seen, the governor, or the president of the council in his absence, was *ex officio* the commander-in-chief. It was his duty to levy, arm and muster all of the able-bodied men of the province, and whenever it became necessary, to use them in putting down insurrections or riots within the colony, in defending the frontiers against invaders, and upon emergencies in aiding the other colonies. It was also his duty to appoint all officers needed in mustering or leading to war, the council always aiding him in this, to build and equip forts, to execute martial law whenever it was deemed necessary, and to keep the board of trade in England informed as to the whole system and its workings. Both the system and his administration of it were to be according to the laws of England and the acts of the provincial assembly, in the passage of which he had much influence.[1] As a rule, the governor did not go into the field as the chief military officer. This position was held by the colonel, lieutenant-colonel or major. The officer in command of the company was the captain, and under him were the adjutant, lieutenant, ensign, corporal and privates.[2]

The system of defence was almost wholly of the militia type, excepting during the fourth intercolonial war. All freemen and men-servants from the age of sixteen to sixty, unless exempted by the laws, were required to organize and drill, as well as keep themselves supplied with arms and a certain amount of ammunition. They were to be listed and apportioned into companies annually, and these must meet at muster and drill at least four times yearly. The regiment with all

[1] C. R. III, 66–73, 112–13; IV, 550–55; VI, 476–78, 803, 808–10, 831, 1090; VII, 333, 385, 552, 926–27; VIII, 192–93; Law Revisals, passim.
[2] Swann, 215–19.

its companies must perform the same duty once a year. The penalty for neglect was twenty pounds for each occurrence upon the colonel and five upon the captain, with a smaller amount for the private. There were some exemptions from muster, but none when actual war came on; and the principle of these changed little during the whole period, being for the most part upon the grounds of public service. Ministers of the Anglican church, members of the council and of the lower house of the legislature, the secretary and the attorney-general of the province, practicing attorneys, and those having served as field officers or captains of the militia, were allowed this privilege. During a part of the period physicians, clerks of the courts of justice, justices of the peace and attendants at public mills or ferries, were given the same immunities. When actual war came all able-bodied men of the legal age, whether free or slave, whether exempted from musters or not, might be called into the field. When once in the army mutiny and desertion were to be punished by a court martial. The composition of the court was provided for by the legislature. While the provincial government made these requirements upon the colonists, it on the other hand provided compensation, by establishing a pension system for the wounded and for the families of the killed.[1]

Such was the system in outline, changing only slightly throughout the colonial period after 1715. From 1663 to 1715 what system there was—exactly what it was we do not know—was very poorly carried

[1] Swann, 215–19.

out. It is most probable that during these years whatever plan there was depended more upon the constantly changing wishes of the proprietors than upon specific acts of the provincial legislature. The proprietors by their charters had all the powers and duties of a captain-general in England, and in 1667 they conferred these upon their governor, giving him the title of commander-in-chief. He was instructed to organize companies for defence, internal and external.[1] Early in the period the proprietors instituted the policy of granting lands upon the freest terms to settlers who would bring with them a certain amount of equipment for defence.[2] But in spite of this provision and of the fact that the colony had located within itself several Indian tribes, and consequently had great need of a system of defence, very little was done for an efficient one prior to 1715. As we have seen, the province was frequently under weak and careless governors or deputy governors, and much disorder prevailed at many different times. As a matter of fact the system of defence under these was neglected to a great degree, mustering and drilling being almost unknown. The anarchy of the period 1705–1711 was so great and the defence so poor that the Tuscarora war left the province almost in desolation and ruin, coming at a time when one portion was arrayed against another, when provincial patriotism was almost gone. Though the Tuscaroras had only twelve hundred fighting men, still so weak and poor was the defence that even this small

[1] C. R. I, 31, 112, 169, 232–33, 239, 361, 389.
[2] C. R. I, 45, 169, et seq.

force could not be successfully met; the colony would have been ruined had not aid arrived from South Carolina.[1]

The disastrous effects of this war demonstrated to the proprietors and colonists alike that their whole system of defence must be reorganized and more carefully executed. This was to be done by the act of 1715–1716, which was in part a revisal of an old one. By this, mustering and training were to be looked after carefully, and consequently the system would be greatly improved. This act became the real foundation of the system for the whole period of the royal administration; the militia was now placed upon a definite footing. For several years after the passage of this act because of the fear of another Indian war musters and drills were held according to its provisions. But soon the time came when the Tuscaroras left the province to join their kindred tribes in New York. Then the Indians were no longer strong enough to be at all dangerous to the colonists and the provisions of the act of 1715–1716 were allowed to go unenforced. The act itself, however, remained unchanged until 1740, then being modified only slightly. Again it was to be changed, though only in some minor points, six years later. This act of 1746 was so typical of the whole period that its provisions have been given in the general outline of the system which has already been described.[2] Three years later when war appeared to be very dis-

[1] C. R. I, passim; Hawks II, 171–72, 390–400, 519–53; Mill's Statistics of South Carolina, 223.

[2] Swann, 6, 215–19; MS. Laws.

tant, even when it was hoped that it would not come again in a long time, the militia law was changed into a less rigid one. Two musters of the companies were now to be held yearly in the place of four, and the death penalty could no longer be applied by the court martial.[1] But the expectations of a long peace were to be disappointed; North Carolina was soon to take part in the fourth inter-colonial war, the longest and greatest one in its history as a province. As a result of this four militia acts were passed. Those of 1756 and 1759 continued the system of 1746 with slight amendments, for the first time making provision for the militia to march out of the colony to the aid of her neighbors. According to the former laws it was to remain in the province and to be used purely as a means of local defence.[2] In 1760 the principle of exemption from musters was extended. Now Presbyterian ministers of regular churches, inspectors of public warehouses, and overseers having under their care as many as six slaves, were to be added to the list which was arranged in 1746. It was extended again in 1762, to coroners and constables, in 1764 to school masters of at least ten pupils, to overseers of the public roads and pilots on the rivers, and in 1770 to Quakers, for a term of five years.[3]

The proprietors and the provincial assembly not only provided for a better system of militia after 1715 but also levied a tax upon all vessels bringing goods into

[1] Swann, 305–06.

[2] Davis, 1765, II, 80, 167; MS. Laws.

[3] Davis, 1765, II, 192–97, 212, 281, 309–15; Davis, 1773, 345, 426, 435–39; C. R. V, 291, 506, 538; IX, 176–77.

the ports of the province for the purpose of establishing and maintaining a magazine of ammunition; and this was continued on far into the royal period.[1] For the support of such a magazine on the frontier, a tax was laid in 1743 upon all the taxables of the counties in which this should be located.[2] Something was done also for the coast defence. The first attempt to fortify this was in 1745 when the Spanish and French vessels were threatening it. Now an act was passed for building a fort on the lower Cape Fear River. This was to be supplied with ammunition by a powder duty laid on imported goods.[3] Three years later the legislature appropriated a very considerable amount for the erection and equipment of four forts along the sea-coast, but only two of these were ever constructed—Fort Johnston at the mouth of the Cape Fear River and Fort Granville at Ocracock, near the middle of the coast line.[4] Though these were built by 1755, they were of little service. They never had much of an equipment, and the expected attacks of the French fleet never came. During the latter part of 1755 an act was passed for erecting and equipping Fort Dobbs on the western frontier, to be used against the Indians. This was built during the next year and was of much service in defending the colonists in the western part of the province.[5]

[1] Swann, 16, 266; MS. Laws.
[2] Swann, 184; MS. Laws.
[3] Swann, 199–201.
[4] Swann, 199–200; Davis, 1765, II, 143–47; C. R. IV, 922–23; V, 18–19.
[5] C. R. V, 157–60, 419–20, 570–71, 593–99, 638–39; Davis, 1765, II, 60; MS. Laws; Waddell, 31–33.

There was something of a semblance of a naval station for the province during the later part of its history. As early as 1740 a request was made by the colonial officers for a man-of-war to be stationed off the coast, near the mouth of the Cape Fear River. Whether this request was ever granted we do not know. In 1757 a twenty gun ship and a sloop were ordered to the province for the protection of the coast against pirates, but that they came there is no evidence. Sometime prior to this a man-of-war was ordered to be stationed at the mouth of the Cape Fear River, but Dobbs in 1757 stated that it had not been at this place more than ten days in three years. Ten years later the sloop Martin was in station off the coast, while in 1775 the sloop Cruizer was in the Cape Fear River, possibly stationed there.[1]

Upon the grounds of efficiency not very much can be said to the credit of the system or of its administration. As we have seen, during the larger part of the proprietary period it was very poor. The proprietors through their officers in the province exercised a rather weak control over the colonists, as the colonists had little respect for the government imposed upon them. With this state of affairs an efficient system of defence was out of the question. The colonists, to be sure, had for the most part the required arms and ammunition, but muster and drill they did not, and to unite all of the forces even in great emergencies was almost impossible. As has been stated, factional feeling and

[1] C. R. IV, 478; V, 748, 792, 963; VI, 51–52, 522, 566–67, 734; VII, 534, 795; X, 96–151; State Records I, 109–10, 134–35.

bitterness were so great during the Carey insurrection that, when the Tuscarora war came on, union for defence, even of their lives and homes, could not be effected. The governor and council issued many appeals to the colonists, but in vain. The humiliating results of such a war made the colonists ashamed of their conduct and drove them to the establishment of a better system of defence, especially to a more rigid execution of it. Further attacks by the Indians were expected for the next five years and this expectation greatly stimulated the spirit of union and of mustering. From this time to the end of the royal period there was a well-defined system, and this was more or less in operation. As this was largely formulated by the colonists in their legislature and as it had incorporated within itself much of their spirit, it received their support to a very considerable degree. Mustering was not, however, at all regular except under the fear of danger; from 1720 to 1740, when there was little probability of attacks by Indians or invasions by the French or Spanish, meetings for drill were very seldom. However, from 1740 to 1748 and again from 1755 to 1763, while war was either at hand or approaching, much attention was given to defence, both in shaping the system to meet the demands and in its proper execution.[1]

The militia for the larger part of the colonial period constituted the system of local defence. The proprietors had no army with which to protect their province and under the crown's administration the royal forces

[1] C. R. III, 153, 433; IV, 243; V, 123–24, 570–71, 575–76, 603–04; VIII, 30–31.

never at any time gave assistance to North Carolina. During the first fifty years the colony had no enemies excepting the Indians, and only one tribe of these was at all strong—the Tuscaroras. It consequently had little actual need of a military force, none until 1711–1713. When war came on the militia, being so poorly trained and the colonists so much divided, could not successfully meet a small Indian force and was not, therefore, able to protect the colonists or their property from devastation and ruin. This first test of the strength of the militia as a means of local defence was, therefore, very unfavorable. From the end of the Tuscarora war to the beginning of the fourth intercolonial struggle, in 1754, the militia was not called into the field for actual service in the defence of the province; it was only for musters. By this time, however, the Cherokees and Catawbas were becoming numerous and threatening on the western frontier, and some means of defence must be provided against them. The colonists in the western counties were too poor to provide for themselves efficient defence and the legislature was called on for aid. In 1754 it voted one thousand pounds to be spent in the purchase of arms and ammunition for these counties, the frontiersmen themselves as militia being asked to supply the service.[1] But early in the next year it was seen that something more must be done, and three thousand pounds were granted for the purpose of raising and equipping a company of soldiers to be used in defending the frontier against the Indians.[2]

[1] Davis, 1765, II, 18–25.
[2] Davis, 1765, II, 35; MS. Laws.

12

During the latter part of the same year another movement was made toward defence in the same locality, money being voted for the erection and equipment of a small fort.[1] When this was erected, it was seen that more soldiers must be stationed at or near it, and during 1756 appropriations were made for raising, equipping and paying two companies for this purpose.[2] These were raised, and they, with the militia of the counties of Rowan, Anson and Orange, defended the frontier against the Indians. They during the fourth intercolonial war were in great agitation against the English, being stirred up by the French.[3] At the end of this war Fort Dobbs was allowed to go to ruin and the defence of the frontier was discontinued, as the Indians were very quiet and peaceful.[4] As we have seen, there were two forts on the coast—Johnston and Granville, which were erected by the beginning of the fourth intercolonial struggle. Although Fort Johnston was partially equipped and continued so to the end of the royal government, Granville was never a fort except in name and after 1763 was wholly abandoned.[5]

The provincial system was used also as a means of the British colonial defence, and much more at times for this than for local purposes. It was not, however, the militia as a rule which was employed in this defence,

[1] Davis, 1765, II, 60; MS. Laws; C. R. V, 638–39.
[2] Davis, 1765, II, 80; C. R. V, 792.
[3] Waddell, 64–66, C. R. V, 50; VI, 229–30.
[4] C. R. VII, 203.
[5] Davis, 1765, II, 143–47; Iredell, 115–17; C. R. V, 18–19, 792, 934; VI, 830–31, 1255; VII, 40, 203, 245–46, 559–60, 863, 902; VIII, 30–31 412, 574–611; IX, 44, 46, 171, 328, 869, 1204, 1221.

but hired volunteers. In 1715 North Carolina sent soldiers to aid South Carolina against the Indians. This was done largely as a return for the assistance which South Carolina had rendered during the Tuscarora war,[1] and was, therefore, not at the request of the crown. It was not until 1740 that the crown made its first demand upon the colony for aid to the general defence, at this time to be employed against the Spanish. The assembly gave great consideration to such a request and granted four hundred soldiers, with commodities for their support and transportation. These with the troops furnished by Virginia and South Carolina for the same purpose made an ineffectual attack upon the Spanish stronghold in Florida—Saint Augustine—and in 1741 were transported to Jamaica, from whence they took part in the disastrous campaign of Admiral Vernon against Carthagena.[2]

From this time until 1754 the province did not aid in the British defence or that of its neighbors. But with the beginning of the fourth intercolonial war many demands began to be made upon it and most of them were granted. In 1754, at the call of the governor of Virginia, the assembly voted seven hundred and fifty soldiers, with twelve thousand pounds for raising and equipping them, to be used in defence of Virginia and of the British interests, which were now being endangered by the French and Indians. This was done with the understanding that Virginia would support them after their arrival within her borders, as they were

[1] Hawks, II, 554.

[2] C. R. IV, 421, 552–58; Swann, 119–25; Martin, II, 30–35.

chiefly for her defence. Upon this point of their support a dispute arose and Virginia refused to supply them with provisions. The number was in consequence reduced to four hundred and fifty. North Carolina, having no coin and a paper currency worthless outside the province, was compelled to send cattle and other provisions for their support. After arriving in Virginia they rendered practically no aid. They receiving no pay from either province and not having sufficient supplies, many deserted. Finally in August of the same year they were disbanded.[1] While this first attempt to aid in fighting the French and Indians failed, still early in the next year a company of one hundred men was sent to Virginia and became a support to General Braddock, the commander of the British colonial forces. During the latter part of the same year nine thousand pounds and one hundred and fifty men, exclusive of officers, were granted by the assembly for the assistance of the colonies to the north, to be used as the governor deemed best.[2] Whether these three companies of fifty men each were sent along with a fourth one of the same size to New York, during the early part of 1756, we cannot say with absolute certainty, though most probably they were.[3] During the first months of the next year, the governors of North Carolina, Virginia, Maryland and Pennsylvania having met at the call of the Earl of Loudon, the com-

---

[1] Davis, 1765, II, 18–25; Swann, 216–17; C. R. V, 11, 109–12, 123–28, 137, 144c, 147, 739; Waddell, 42–48.

[2] C. R. V, 366–72, 401–02, 601, 739; MS. Laws; Waddell, 55.

[3] C. R. V, 601, 739.

mander-in-chief of the crown's forces in North America, devised a plan for the defence of the Southern Colonies. Upon these provinces doing their part the crown promised to send to their aid a battalion of soldiers, with supplies and munitions of war. The center of this campaign was to be South Carolina, against the southern Indians. North Carolina, in order to aid her neighbor and the British interests, very willingly granted the demands made upon her for two hundred fighting men, with pay and with supplies until they should arrive in South Carolina. The crown had agreed to provide for their necessities after they were placed under a British commander.[1] Within a few months Major Waddell was placed in command of three companies of one hundred men each. These, with seven thousand pounds for their pay and equipment, were granted by the assembly for the final attack upon Fort DuQuesne.[2]

By the end of 1758 North Carolina had granted to the crown for the purpose of carrying on the fourth intercolonial war more than sixty-six thousand pounds, and more than thirty-eight thousand of this had been used outside of the province—that is for the British colonial defence.[3] But this was not all that North Carolina did in this war. As we have seen, she furnished a fair number of soldiers from 1754 to 1759, and after this until the end of the struggle she con-

[1] C. R. V, 744, 750–52, 762; Davis, 1765, II, 120; MS. Laws.

[2] C. R. V, 934, 1010; Davis, 1765, II, 136; MS. Laws; Waddell, 39, 56–63.

[3] C. R. V, 986–87.

tinued to grant both troops and money. The Cherokees were now becoming very restless and threatening,
especially against South Carolina. They, in pursu-
ance of a treaty made with England, had been quiet for
the past three years, but in 1758–1759 they assumed a
very hostile attitude. Under these conditions the governor of South Carolina called on Georgia and her two
neighbors to the north for aid. During 1759 Colonel
Waddell (now of this rank) was ordered to lead the
provincials in the pay of the province and as many as
five hundred of the militia of Anson, Rowan and
Orange counties to the assistance of South Carolina,
a small sum being voted for their transportation.[1]
The militia refused to go, however, on the ground that
they by law were to be used only for the defence of
their own province. The assembly, being appealed to,
changed the militia act so as to require them to go outside of the province in cases of great emergencies.[2] In
addition to sending these provincials and militia, the
assembly during the early part of the next year appropriated five thousand pounds for paying and supporting these while in service.[3] Again in June of the same
year it granted seven thousand pounds for raising and
paying three companies to be in service until December, 1760. But by the end of this year the war was not
yet over; the Cherokees were still in a threatening attitude, especially toward South Carolina. England now
planned to attack these with the provincial forces of

[1] C. R. V, 61, 125; Davis, 1765, II, 167; MS. Laws; Waddell, 64–65.
[2] C. R. VI, 112, 220–21; MS. Laws; Waddell, 65.
[3] C. R. VI, 125; Davis, 1765, II, 167; MS. Laws.

Virginia and the two Carolinas.[1] Though this plan was wholly successful in bringing the Indians to terms, still North Carolina continued to grant soldiers and supplies for the interests of the British colonial policy. In March, 1761, she granted money sufficient, at least it was thought so, to raise, clothe and pay five hundred men, to be used as the governor of the province or the commander-in-chief of the king's forces in North America deemed best.[2] But this was the last grant which the assembly would allow, and this too in spite of another request for men and money from the British military commander. Early in 1762 General Amherst made a requisition upon the province for one hundred and thirty-four soldiers, exclusive of officers, but the assembly refused to pass any act to this effect. However, the governor acknowledged the request, and ordered that these be raised and that they be paid out of the province's part of the appropriations made by the British parliament.[3]

From first to last, therefore, North Carolina spent a large amount in the fourth intercolonial war, a good deal for her own defence, but much more in aid of the British policy and interests. At one time the English parliament voted fifty thousand pounds in partial repayment to Virginia and the two Carolinas, and at another two hundred thousand pounds to be distributed among all of the colonies. Of these two appropriations North Carolina received only 7,789 pounds, while

[1] C. R. VI, 266, 324–26; Davis, 1765, II, 189–92; Iredell, 193.
[2] Davis, 1765, II, 220–23; Iredell, 198–200.
[3] C. R. VI, 705; Martin, II, 181.

Virginia received about seven times as much.[1] This dividend to North Carolina appears to be only a small part of what the province had paid out, but in reality it was much larger than it at first sight appears; the large amount appropriated by the assembly was in colonial currency and this, as we have seen, was greatly depreciated, passing at a very great discount. Still for the most part North Carolina had discharged well her duty in this war. But as we have seen, she took no part whatever in the first three intercolonial wars. In fact she was far separated from the French and to a large extent from the Indians who were under the French influence, and there was, therefore, no great stimulus to take a very active or extensive part in these conflicts. They were upon a small scale and were confined to the colonies of the north. North Carolina was not alone in her conduct during the first three wars between the English and the French in North America; her neighbors neither took any interest worth consideration nor sent aid of a very important kind.

As we have seen, the system of defence under the crown did not become of fundamental and vital importance until 1754, and, therefore, did not play an active part in the politics of the province prior to this time. But from 1754 to 1763 matters of defence became the absorbing question. Governor Dobbs began his administration in 1754 under the most auspicious and pleasant relations between himself and the provincial assembly. It appeared that under him the col-

[1] C. R. VI, 285–87; preface, pp. x–xii.

onists and the crown officers placed over them would continue to cherish the most cordial feelings toward each other. But troubles came thick and fast upon the colony. The French and the Indians were putting forth their greatest energies to make encroachments, and the province must defend itself, as well as lend aid to its sister colonies in keeping back these encroachments and in subduing their rivals. Dobbs as the chief executive must call upon the assembly for men and money, and so frequently was he compelled to do this that it began to complain of his administration, though it was in the main successful. Although several quarrels occurred between the governor and the assembly over these calls for money, still the requests were granted throughout the period until near its close. Only once, in 1762, as we have seen, did the assembly refuse outright to vote such a request. But though it granted the requests, in almost every instance of granting aid it gained something in the way of privileges for itself; in fact very frequently its grants were purchased by these privileges.

CHAPTER IX.

THE CONFLICTS BETWEEN THE EXECUTIVE AND THE LOWER HOUSE UNDER THE CROWN.

THE functions and relations of the governor, council and lower house of the legislature have already been considered. The executive, the governor and the council, directly representing the crown, was very naturally disposed to look to its interests, even to the disadvantage of the colonists. It was its special duty to administer the affairs of the province in a manner that would bring the best possible results to the crown; and a model government of an English royal province in the eighteenth century was one which aimed to add much to the material advantage of the government and people of England. The lower house of the legislature represented the colonists, who were likewise working for their own interests. They could never fully understand or appreciate the significance and benefits of the crown's government. In theory they were protected by the king; in reality they to a large extent protected themselves. While the colonists never fully understood the policy of the home government, it is equally true that the people and officials in England knew very little about the ideas and sentiments of the farmers of North Carolina. Under these conditions, and with the organization and powers which the executive and lower

186

house had, it was natural that they should come into conflicts of a fundamental and serious nature.

There were some disputes between these departments on really trivial and personal matters, and some of these hindered the cause of good government. The larger number of the conflicts were on constitutional and vital points. It was on questions of land and quit-rents, fees, money and the treasurers, the agent, courts and judges, that these conflicts became important and serious. In this connection the more formal or consti-tutional aspects of the conflicts and disputes upon ques-tions of land, money and justice will be considered; elsewhere the details of these disputes have been given and discussed. The following discussion will be made for the specific purpose of showing what the positions of the executive and the lower house were upon the most vital questions of government, with the convic-tion that when these positions are clearly compre-hended the most difficult problem in the history of North Carolina as a royal province will be practically solved.

The conflicts arising from the different points of view concerning the administration of the territorial system came into prominence early in 1731, and Gov-ernor Burrington and the lower house could never come to an agreement upon them. In April of this year the lower house, after considering the instructions from the crown concerning the payment of quit-rents, adopted a resolution to the effect that there was not coin enough in the province with which to pay one half of the rents, and that, therefore, such payment should

188   NORTH CAROLINA

be made in valuable commodities or bills, at a proper rate of exchange. The governor insisted that the payment should be made in coin or in bills at a very low rate of exchange, and that payment in commodities and bills at the rate which the house had assigned was to the great disadvantage of the crown. The lower house valued the commodities at high rates and demanded that the provincial bills be accepted at a small discount. During May of the same year a conference was held between the two parties in the dispute, but neither one yielding it accomplished nothing. Both Burrington and the representatives gave evidences of much bad feeling and no agreement could be reached.[1]

During the assembly of 1733 these questions became the subject of a more bitter dispute than had occurred in Burrington's first legislature. The lower house still demanded that quit-rents should be paid in commodities at high rates and in bills at a small discount, while Burrington maintained that the rents were due in sterling and that its claims were based upon mere assumptions. The tone of his speeches, as well as his demands, were such as to cause the struggle to continue. The lower house in defending its position finally made the claim that the deed of 1668 from the proprietors, known as the "original deed," was a permanent and binding document, and that, therefore, the crown had no right to give instructions concerning quit-rents which were contrary to this deed.[2] This claim, which practically denied the crown's right of regulating the territorial

[1] C. R. III, 143–44, 157–68, 279–80, 294.
[2] C. R. III, 598–99, 606–09, 621.

system, had no legal or constitutional basis, and it was, as Burrington characterized it, a mere assumption of power. During the proprietary period the colonists had enjoyed certain privileges concerning their lands, and these were and ought to have been respected by the crown. But to deny the crown the right to modify them in the slightest degree was the assumption by the lower house of absolute independence. In their demands concerning the payment of quit-rents in commodities at high rates and in bills at a small discount they were ignoring the rights of the crown and depriving it of some of its legitimate dues, and the governor in refusing to assent to such demands was doing his duty. But on the other hand he was going to extremes in claiming that quit-rents should be paid in sterling only. The colonists had very little coin, and to demand rents in sterling only was a hardship to them and a mistake on the part of the executive.

Governor Johnston, as well as his predecessor, had some conflicts with the lower house on questions relating to land, but these never become so serious as to prevent any legislation whatever on the subject. Under him seven territorial acts were passed, but two of these were disallowed by the crown because of clauses which were derogatory to the interests of the home government.[1] This would indicate that Johnston was more compromising than Burrington, and affords a partial explanation of the fact that his conflicts with the lower house were not so serious as those under Burrington. While not so serious as under Burrington,

[1] Swann, passim.

still the disputes of Johnston with the lower house came from the same causes. Early in 1735 the lower house in replying to him stated that when the province was granted by the crown to the proprietors, they were given the power to grant lands to all inhabitants at such rents as they could agree upon; that the proprietors through their governors, the council and the lower house, were to make all the laws concerning land, which should be binding on the proprietors and their tenants; that by the "original deed" of 1668 the proprietors gave to their governor and council the power of granting lands in North Carolina upon the same terms as lands were granted in Virginia, at two shillings per one hundred acres, payable in tobacco at one penny per pound; that when it was discovered that North Carolina could not produce as good tobacco as Virginia the payment was changed from tobacco to other commodities at certain rates, at which rates the commodities had always been received by the proprietors; and that for these reasons it was proper to claim that the "original deed" was still in force, though all the other proprietary laws had become void. It also declared that the governor's demand that quit-rents be paid in sterling was contrary to this deed from the proprietors, and, therefore, illegal. It asked the governor to have the rents collected according to the customs of the province until a law could be secured to that effect.[1]

On the same day Johnston sent the lower house a message, in which he declared that its ideas concerning

_____
[1] C. R. IV, 109–10.

quit-rents were contrary to the king's rights and privileges. He argued that the "original deed" from the proprietors contained nothing which made it irrevocable, and that it had actually been revoked by the proprietors in 1670, when they gave another deed, which required the payment of quit-rents in coin at one half penny per acre, and that the acts directing the payment in commodities had never received the assent of the proprietors and consequently had not become laws. He further stated that North Carolina had adopted the crown laws when she became a royal province.[1] His argument, though to a very great extent historically and legally sound, did not convince the members of the house, and no act was passed and agreed to at this assembly.[2]

Thus the position which the lower house took under Burrington and Johnston in regard to matters of land was in many respects illegal and against the interests of the crown. It was its right and duty to see that the territorial administration was for the true welfare of the province, but there was no justification in its demanding that the interests of the crown should be ignored or harmed.

By the time that Dobbs became governor, territorial questions had come to assume far less importance, hence they were no longer the subject of conflicts between the governor and the lower house. Military, judicial and fiscal problems were now the chief ones and upon these came the conflicts after 1754.

[1] C. R. IV, 110–14.
[2] C. R. IV, 8.

Not only did the governor and the lower house become involved in disputes over the territorial system, but the council and the lower house did likewise. From 1735 to 1740 bills relating to quit-rents were the causes of much dispute between the two houses. The lower house attempted to frame them so that their execution would impose as little a burden as possible upon the colonists, and at times almost ignored the rights of the crown. The upper house refused to agree to such action; it maintained, as far as it could, the rights and privileges of the crown. During February, 1735, the lower house sent a message to the upper house in regard to a bill for quit-rents. It stated that the upper house had amended its bill so as to restrict the payment of quit-rents to only four places, and claimed that this would be a heavy burden to the colonists, that rents were payable on the land unless expressly stated otherwise, and that such had been the custom in North Carolina, South Carolina and Virginia. The bill of the lower house proposed that rents be paid in the best possible commodities and at several places on the navigable rivers, no allowance being made for carriage.[1] The upper house replied that it was compelled to reject the bill because of the many clauses which were against the crown's rights and interests. It said that the bill of the lower house would compel the crown to spend one half of its quit-rents in collecting them, and that this was unfair and illegal.[2] No agreement was reached at this session. These questions were

[1] C. R. IV, 132–33.
[2] C. R. IV, 133–35.

again much discussed and were the causes of conflicts in the assembly of October, 1736. At this session another bill for quit-rents was rejected by the upper house and for reasons similar to those mentioned above.[1] In February, 1739, after some dispute concerning the force of the "original deed," the payment in sterling and commodities, and other detailed points, the two houses came to an agreement, each yielding on some points to the other.[2] After 1740 the records give no evidence of important conflicts between the two branches of the legislature on territorial questions. In those which occurred from 1735 to 1740 the upper house had taken substantially the same position as the governor in his conflicts with the lower house; the executive —the governor and the council—was, therefore, practically a unit in this.

The governor and the lower house, while acting much more harmoniously on the questions of fees than on land, still became involved in some conflicts concerning them. In April, 1731, Burrington sent a paper to the lower house in which he claimed that its charges that fees were much higher in North Carolina than in Virginia, were unreasonable and false. This made the representatives angry and they in turn sent him a reply, in which they declared that for nearly twenty years, according to old customs and laws, officers had been paid in paper currency and at rates established by the lower house. They stated that officers under the crown were taking four times as much in fees as those under the

---

[1] C. R. IV, 240.
[2] C. R. IV, 368–69, 373.

13

proprietors had done, and in a bitter tone made many complaints about his whole administration. He in reply advanced the claim that he and the council alone had the full power to establish and regulate fees, and that the king's instructions, which stated that all fees should be paid in proclamation money, repealed all the proprietary laws concerning fees.[1] This claim on the part of the governor exaggerated his own powers and those of the council, and ignored some of the privileges of the lower house, privileges which it had enjoyed both by direct grants from the proprietors and by allowances on the part of the proprietors. The crown respected many of these privileges, but time and again announced its right to modify them. It is evident that the king intended that the modifications should be made by the governor and council, with the consent of the lower house, if possible. Burrington's claim, therefore, though much exaggerated, had a certain legal basis. But the lower house would not accept his interpretation. It was in a large measure correct in declaring that it, as well as the governor and council, had a right to establish and regulate fees, but in its claim that its privileges from the proprietors could not be modified by the crown it was going too far. Such a claim denied the right of the crown to regulate public matters in its own province, which right the crown had by virtue of the fact that it was the chief executive and the ultimate source of governmental powers in the province.

Burrington asked for a compromise and proposed a conference. A conference was held, but with no results

[1] C. R. III, 95, 103, 265, 267, 270–72.

looking to a compromise. The lower house would not yield to his demand that fees be paid in proclamation money according to the crown's instructions; it insisted upon tobacco and bills of credit being accepted, and upon the right of deciding at what rates these should be received. Burrington was perhaps too obstinate in demanding that fees be paid in proclamation money only. The lower house on the other hand gave little evidence of desiring to do the fair thing when it ordered that fees be accepted in commodities at high rates and in bills at par, which were much depreciated.[1]

Under Johnston fees brought on no serious dispute. Still he and the lower house had different opinions concerning the amount of fees, in what they should be paid and who had the right of regulating them.[2] However, after 1736 there is practically no evidence of a conflict over these, excepting once, in 1760. During May of that year the lower house complained of Dobbs taking too high fees, but this complaint was not well founded, as the records show, and was of no consequence.[3] From 1736 to 1774 the lower house at times made complaints about certain officers taking and demanding exorbitant or illegal fees, but for the most part the governor was as ready as the representatives to correct such abuses; and during this period the evidence, both of a positive and negative nature, would indicate that the governor and the lower house were willing to compromise on fees, as they did on territorial questions. In fact other and

[1] C. R. III, 144, 151–52, 280–81.
[2] C. R. IV, 173–78, 189–200.
[3] C. R. VI, 288–89.

far more important problems were then demanding the attention of both parties.

Fees were the subject of some conflict between the two houses of the legislature. During 1731 the lower house took into consideration the question of regulating fees, and especially in what they should be paid. It complained of the action on the part of the governor and the council in regulating them without its own consent. The council had taken the instructions from the crown, which declared that fees should be payable in proclamation money, as its guide, and it and the governor had acted accordingly. The lower house not only denounced their action, but went so far as to declare such action, though upon the authority of royal instructions, illegal and oppressive. The upper house, or council, was displeased at such a declaration on the part of the lower house, and sent it a resolution in which it was stated that the lower house in making such a declaration was not only invading the crown's prerogative but was divesting the governor and council of their powers which the crown had given them. This caused the lower house to take a more conservative view. It now disavowed its statement concerning the illegality and oppression of the royal instructions. But it still made its own interpretations of the crown's instructions in regard to fees and declared that these were intended to mean that fees should be regulated by colonial acts, in the passage of which it should have as much part as the governor and the upper house. No act concerning fees was passed by this assembly though serious attempts were made to this effect; neither house was willing to yield, at least upon the question as to what fees should be payable in. The lower house insisted upon the use of bills of credit which were much depreciated, while the upper house adhered to the instructions from the crown which called for proclamation money.[1] The upper house was in this, therefore, in substantial sympathy and agreement with the governor.

The conflicts relating to fees did not arise from the institution in itself, but had reference to the form of their payment and the parties who should regulate them; they were, therefore, conflicts arising chiefly from the fiscal side of the system. Both parties, the executive and the lower house, in the main agreed that there should be a system of fees. They were willing to allow certain fees to the governor, the officers in chancery and admiralty, the secretary, chief justice, associate justices, attorney-generals, marshals, collectors of customs, registers, surveyors, escheators, constables, justices of the peace and clerks of the different courts. Fees constituted the chief or only compensation of these officers. On the question that they should be allowed, the executive and the lower house were in agreement, but in regard to some of the details of the system they entertained very different views.[2]

The disposition and control of the public revenue were subjects of much controversy between the gover-

[1] C. R. III, 95, 103, 151–52, 157–68, 264, 269.
[2] C. R. III, 95, 159–68, 188, 265, 267, 270–72, 294, 496–98; IV, 189–98, 446–47; VI, 1097; VII, 796; IX, 165; MS. Laws; Swann, 250–58; Davis, 1765, II, 230–31; Davis, 1773, 456, 473–75, 503–04.

nor and the lower house during the larger part of the royal period. During April, 1731, the lower house in reply to the governor's speech, discussed fiscal matters and declared that no public moneys should be issued except by the governor, council and itself. One of Burrington's instructions directed him to allow no money to be issued or disposed of except by his warrant issued upon the advice of the council, but he was to allow the lower house to review and examine the accounts. This instruction was intended to take the distribution of the public moneys largely from the lower house and to allow it no further control than that which it might have from reviewing the accounts of expenditures. The lower house would not accept such an instruction, at least Burrington's interpretation of it, and claimed that the act of 1715 concerning the public treasurer gave more power than that involved in reviewing and examining accounts. Burrington would not recognize such a claim, and held that his instructions from the crown had legally superseded all the laws of the proprietary period. During his whole administration conflicts upon this subject continued between the lower house and himself. It claimed the privileges which it had enjoyed during the proprietary government, of having a large share in the distribution of public moneys, while he insisted rigidly upon the letter of his instructions concerning their disposition.[2] Not only did the representatives refuse to recognize his claims, but they proceeded to carry their own into action. They appointed

[1] C. R. III, 100, 103, 265.
[2] C. R. III, 265–672, passim.

and, therefore, controlled the public treasurers; they had already, by an act of 1729, which the crown apparently never approved, established the office of treasurer in eleven precincts, and the control of these was within their power.[1] His claim was to a large extent legal, as it was based upon specific instructions from the crown, but his interpretation of his fiscal powers tended to deprive the lower house of privileges which the proprietors had granted or allowed it. The position of the lower house was to an extent extra legal, but when considered in the light of what had been its customary privileges it was not a very extravagant one. The crown, while having the right to modify these privileges, still did not propose to do so in a very violent manner, and, therefore, did not sustain its governor in his extreme position.

According to the records Johnston had few, if any conflicts, on this subject; he apparently yielded to the demands of the lower house. Dobbs had no disputes with it until 1759. From 1759 to 1765 he had some conflicts with it, as he attempted to recover for the crown the control over the fiscal system and its administration. In this he failed, and the authorities at home gave him no encouragement to continue the struggle. The board of trade in writing to him in August, 1759, stated that the custom of the appointment of treasurers by the assembly, or the lower house alone, and of their being amenable to these bodies only had been too long in vogue to be checked.[2] This is fairly good evidence

[1] C. R. III, 151.
[2] C. R. VI, 6, 55.

that the lower house had practically controlled the disposition of public moneys from the beginning of the royal government. Not only did it do this in time of peace, but also during war. From 1754 to 1760 a good many acts were passed, which granted aids to the crown for the purposes of war. This money was not placed under the control of the treasurers, who were directly amenable to the lower house; it was put in the hands of special commissioners, or of the governor, in order that the war measures might be facilitated. However, these aids, though granted to the crown, were really not wholly at the disposal of the crown's agent—the governor. The lower house insisted upon the right of examining all the accounts of the expenditure of such moneys. During May, 1760, it drew up several resolves concerning the fiscal administration of Dobbs during the war and made several charges against him for his failure to render full accounts to it and for his lack of good judgment, as it thought, in applying these moneys.[1] During the latter years of Dobbs' administration the lower house at times went to the extreme of not allowing the governor and the council the right of inspecting the treasurer's accounts.[2] So that Dobbs was almost at the mercy of the representatives in his fiscal administration. He made several attempts to secure partial control of public monies, but failed in each case.

Governor Tryon and the lower house had no conflicts on this question worth special mention. He allowed it to dispose of the public moneys according to the customs

[1] C. R. VI, 280–84, 287–88, 410–13.
[2] C. R. VI, 321.

of the province, provided it would grant him as much as he needed to carry out his extravagant ideas. Still there is some evidence that he and the lower house had fundamentally different ideas as to how the fiscal system should be administered. According to his theories of government the disposition of the public moneys belonged to the executive and not to the lower house of the legislature.[1] The policy of the lower house was to appoint sheriffs and treasurers who should collect and expend the public revenue. In theory, these fiscal officers, being appointed by the lower house, were controlled by it, but in reality they controlled the representatives in many respects. It was to remedy this defect, to deprive the fiscal officers as far as possible of their influence over the legislature, that Tryon urged that the fiscal system be placed under the control of the executive. It was during the latter part of his administration that the lower house advanced further claims concerning money matters, or at least stated old claims in a stronger and more specific manner than it had before. In November, 1769, it resolved that the sole right of imposing taxes upon the people was then and had ever been legally and constitutionally vested in itself.[2] It had already set up the claim that it was entitled to a large share of the control of the public moneys. It now declared that it alone had the right to levy the taxes, the chief source from which the public revenue came.

Governor Martin had to administer the affairs of the province at a time when fiscal conditions were bad, and

[1] C. R. VIII, 104–5.
[2] C. R. VIII, 122.

problems of this nature were therefore important and serious during his administration. In 1772 the lower house passed a bill to the effect that a certain poll tax and excise duty had had their effect and should no longer be collected. Martin rejected the bill, because he did not think that the said tax and duty had been collected in sufficient amounts to discharge the debts for the payment of which they had been levied, as the house declared, and because he desired to regain some control over fiscal affairs; to his mind, filled with the prerogative idea, the lower house should be checked in its assumption of power. It, however, in spite of the rejection of the bill, resolved that the sheriffs and collectors should no longer collect the tax and duty. Martin then appealed to the council, which advised him to issue a proclamation requiring all sheriffs and collectors to continue to collect the said tax and duty under the penalty of being sued on their bonds, and this was done. But the lower house had already provided for an emergency by resolving to indemnify the officers who should obey it and were consequently sued by the governor.[1] Because of this resolution, Martin dissolved the assembly. During December, 1773, this question came up again, and again the governor and the lower house took the same positions that they had taken during the previous assembly. Neither side would yield, and consequently no agreement was reached.[2]

In this struggle the governor was, as far as the records bear testimony, acting according to a sound though

[1] C. R. IX., 228–35.
[2] C. R. IX, 745, 944.

narrow policy. The tax and duty, on which the two
parties became involved in a conflict, were levied by acts
of the assembly for the purpose of redeeming the bills
of credit which were issued in 1748 and 1754. The
lower house in 1772, and again in 1773, declared that
the tax and duty had already had the effect of sinking
the said bills of credit. Such a claim was based upon
either a mistake in calculation or a misunderstanding
of the fiscal acts. According to the acts of 1748, 1754,
1760, and 1761, 93,350 pounds of these bills of credit
were emitted. By 1772, 53,104 pounds of these had
been redeemed and there was cash in the treasury to
the amount of 12,586 pounds to be used for the same
purpose. After this cash had been used in redeeming
bills of credit there would still be outstanding bills to
the amount of 27,660 pounds. To redeem these there
must be some source of revenue, and as the records give
evidence, though not with absolute certainty, the tax
and duty which the lower house resolved to discontinue
were the only sources of income.[1] Martin was, therefore, correct in not yielding to its demands. Though
the authorities in England stood by their governor in
his position,[2] still the representatives were not ready
to yield. No compromise was reached, and both parties
remained hostile to each other. The lower house from
the beginning of the royal govenment had exercised
very considerable fiscal powers. Under Johnston,
Dobbs and Tryon it won additional powers, and under
Martin it assumed a position of practical independence.

[1] C. R. IX, 166–67, 201, 230–35, 744–45.
[2] C. R. IX, 301.

The two houses agreed on many points in the fiscal administration, but from 1744 to 1769 they left evidence of disputes and conflicts. In March, 1744, the problem of redeeming the outstanding currency was one much under discussion between the two branches of the legislature. The upper house declared that the vote of the lower house on this subject and for emitting new bills of credit was contrary to equity in its public debt clause and contrary to good sense as well as equity in its currency clause, though they did not specify in what particulars these clauses were unsound. After much dispute the upper house advised the governor to dissolve the assembly, which he at once did.[1] This question came up again in the November assembly of 1744. The upper house now proposed that the redemption bill which proceeded from the lower house should be amended: (1) that a land tax of six pence per hundred acres be laid as a means of paying the outstanding bills; (2) that two commodities of universal value be taken in payment of the said tax. In addition to these proposed amendments it struck out the clause which allowed wages to the members of the two houses. The lower house insisted upon the clause which provided for the wages of members of the assembly, and refused to accept the amendments of the upper house. It proposed that the outstanding bills be paid by means of a tax on each tithable for a term of eight years. Neither house would yield, and the bill was consequently rejected by the upper house.[2] There seems to have been no con-

[1] C. R. IV, 716–18.
[2] C. R. IV, 746–48, 752, 780, 781.

stitutional reason for these conflicts, except that the lower house claimed that the task of providing for the redemption of the currency, as well as the payment of taxes, should be left to it, and that the council should have nothing to do with either.[1] The payment of wages to both houses alike was certainly not a constitutional question. The difference between a land and a poll tax was not very great and was only a fiscal matter. The fact that the governor took no part in the disputes affords some evidence that they arose chiefly from personal differences.

The two houses became involved in some conflicts over the nomination of public treasurers. The lower house claimed the exclusive right of nominating such officers, while the upper house declared that it had at least equal rights with the lower house in this. In 1750 a long dispute arose over this question, and the upper house rejected a bill appointing a treasurer, after no compromise could be reached.[2] A similar incident occurred in 1765 and with the same results.[3] During 1766 this question was raised again, but after considerable discussion the upper house yielded to the claims of the lower house.[4] In this struggle the council was maintaining the legal rights of the crown, the governor and itself, as opposed to the action of the lower house, but in the end it yielded and allowed the representatives of the people almost complete control over the fiscal system.

[1] C. R. IV, 780–81.
[2] C. R. IV, 1058–59, 1061.
[3] C. R. VII, 56.
[4] C. R. VII, 312–14, 324, 330.

The appointment and control of an agent in England was a matter of importance and was a subject of controversy during the years 1759 to 1761. The lower house won in its struggle with the governor, and the authorities in England granted most of its claims. The first conflict occurred in January, 1759. The lower house then passed a bill in which an agent was appointed and provided for, and, in order to compel the council and governor to assent to its bill, it refused to act on other matters until such assent was obtained. Dobbs, rather than yield to the claims of the lower house, prorogued the assembly.[1] In May of the same year he asked the legislature for a supply bill for the purposes of war, but it refused to pass this unless the governor would allow it to designate an agent in the bill. This he refused to do on the ground that such action, as he thought, took away the king's prerogative.[2] However, the board of trade, in writing to Dobbs during the latter part of 1759, stated that they approved of his rejecting the said bill, but that it did not infringe on the king's prerogative and rights as much as he thought. They stated that the method followed by the lower house in appointing an agent was in the main proper and had been allowed by the crown in the Jamaica case; and that, while the governor should see to it that the laws of the provincial legislature secured his majesty's rights, they did not think he should have dissolved the assembly because of its action in this matter.[3] During the first session

[1] C. R. VI, 2-3.
[2] C. R. VI, 32-40.
[3] C. R. VI, 54-56.

of the legislature of 1760 this question came up again, and neither side was willing to compromise. The lower house passed a bill appointing a Mr. Bacon as agent, but the upper house refused to accept him. The lower house then declared that it alone had the right of appointing and instructing the agent, and could do it independently of the council and governor. For such a declaration the governor dissolved the assembly.[1] But the authorities in England again expressed their disapproval of the action of Dobbs. In April, 1761, the board of trade in writing to him stated that he had hindered his majesty's service and that of South Carolina, by his trivial policy in insisting on his rights concerning the appointment of an agent, and in rejecting an aid bill because it contained an agent clause. They stated that the people through their representatives had the right of nominating an agent; that the only thing of which he could legally object in their appointment was the mode thereof, and that, while the lower house acted contrary to custom in doing this in a supply bill, his rejection of the bill for that reason was trivial.[2]

The question of the agent was also the subject of conflicts between the two houses. These began in 1759 and continued to be of some importance until 1769. The lower house claimed the larger share in the appointment and control of the agent, and that such was an inherent and undoubted right of its own. The upper house refused to approve such a claim and rejected several bills for the appointment of agents be-

[1] C. R. VI, 345, 417.
[2] C. R. VI, 538–41.

cause they contained provisions asserting it.[1] The position of the council was thus practically the same as that of the governor. The executive desired to retain as much control over the agent as possible. It was anxious to have an officer residing in London who would represent its side with fullness and sympathy. The lower house for a similar reason desired that its control should be supreme. The appointment of such an agent was, therefore, a matter of importance to both parties. From the practical point of view the lower house was more nearly correct in its demands than the governor. He had ready means of communication with the home government without such an agent; it was also his specific duty to communicate with the board of trade and secretary of state concerning all provincial matters, while the lower house could not obtain a hearing of its case before the authorities in England unless through the governor or an agent. When the governor was hostile it was not likely that he would adequately represent its cause. So that, as a matter of necessity, the lower house demanded that the province should keep an agent in London and that it, as representing the colonists, should have the larger control over him. The board of trade recognized the justice of such claims and directed the governor to grant most of them.

It was upon judicial problems, as upon fiscal questions, that the struggles betweeen the governor and the lower house became great and serious; the conflicts over land, fees and the agent were of minor importance as compared with these. It was not until 1760 that

[1] C. R. VI, 92–93, 423–24, 1136–37, 1141–44, 1286–88; VIII, 11.

judicial problems became so important. It is true that before this time there had been a judicial system under the control of the crown, but this was not the subject of any conflicts worth mentioning. But between 1760 and 1763, and 1773 and 1775, these problems were much discussed and debated. The lower house during May, 1760, presented to Dobbs a bill for the establishment of superior courts of pleas and grand sessions. He rejected it, and then laid the bill and some of his instructions before the chief justice for an opinion. He was instructed not to appoint any person to be judge or justice of the peace without the advice and consent of at least three councillors signified in a council meeting, and that all commissions to judges or justices of the peace be during pleasure only. Dobbs claimed that the bill violated the crown's rights as expressed in the said instructions. By this bill associate justices were nominated, whose commissions were to be given *quamdiu se bene gesserint*. The bill stated nothing about the chief justice, as he was appointed by the crown but with a commission during pleasure only. Dobbs argued that the lower house in nominating the associate justice had taken from him and the council the right of appointing justices, and that the clause which made the commissions during good behavior was an open violation of the rights of the crown. This argument, though legally sound, did not convince the chief justice that the bill should be rejected. He advised the governor that the said bill, while it contained some rather strange ideas, should be accepted, as it was the best possible

14

under the circumstances.[1] Neither did the governor's argument cause the lower house to change its position, and the struggle was kept up. But the province in the meantime fell into great disorder because of a lack of courts, and by the end of 1762 Dobbs assented to bills for superior and inferior courts for two years, in spite of several objectionable clauses.[2]

Between 1763 and 1773 questions affecting the judiciary did not occupy the attention of the governor and the lower house, but from 1773 to 1775 these were again among the chief causes of conflict. During February, 1773, the lower house presented to Martin a bill amending and continuing the act of 1768 for superior courts. He thought it derogatory to the rights of the crown and rejected it.[3] A new bill relating to superior and inferior courts was then introduced and passed, though with a clause suspending its operation till the king should express his wishes. Owing to the pressure of circumstances, Martin gave his assent to this, notwithstanding it contained several objectionable clauses. When this act was sent to England, Richard Jackson, at the request of the board of trade, examined it. He in a report to the board stated that it contained two objectionable points: (1) that relating to the legal process of attaching the goods of a person not residing in the province; (2) that which limited the original jurisdiction of the superior courts to debts and demands amounting to not less than fifty pounds proclamation

[1] C. R. VI, 246–48, 252–54, 361–62, 402–04, 408–9, 413–17.
[2] C. R. VI, 890–92, 970.
[3] C. R. IX, 534.

money when the plaintiff and defendant both resided
in the same district, and to not less than twenty-
five pounds when they resided in different districts.
He further stated that the clause granting an attachment of the goods of persons not residing in
North Carolina was specifically in violation of royal
instructions, though he did not state exactly what these
were, and consequently advised the disallowance of the
act.[1] By this act the lower house attempted to give the
province substantially all the powers of attachment
which belonged to a sovereign state and to extend the
jurisdiction of the inferior or lower courts. In regulating the superior courts the lower house was always
limited by the fact that the chief justice was appointed
by the crown and was, therefore, responsible to the home
government. But in regard to the inferior courts there
were few legal limitations upon the representatives.
By this act the jurisdiction of the lower courts was extended while that of the superior courts was limited.
This was an attempt on the part of the lower house to
extend its regulation over a large part of the judicial
affairs. The lower courts were much more under its
direction than the higher courts, and to extend their
jurisdiction meant a further extension of the powers
of the lower house. The superior courts were to a very
considerable extent under the control of the crown and,
therefore, to limit their jurisdiction was to take power
away from the crown. It was perfectly natural, therefore, that Martin should oppose such assumption of
power and that the crown should not allow it.

[1] C. R. IX, 670.

In December, 1773, Martin, in his opening speech, stated that the crown had disallowed the act mentioned above, chiefly because of the foreign attachment clause. He also stated that the king deemed the extension of the jurisdiction of the inferior courts to cases of fifty pounds inadmissable. On the other hand, he assured the lower house that the king was willing to allow a provision for attachment in cases where the action should arise in the province, which was customary in the commercial cities of continental Europe.[1] At the same time he informed the lower house that he had been compelled by unfavorable circumstances and the lack of courts to appoint a court of oyer and terminer and general jail delivery for the trial of the many criminals then in prison. The disallowance of its act by the crown and the appointment of special courts by the governor caused the lower house to take a still stronger position. It would not yield to a change in its ideas respecting attachment and held that commissions of oyer and terminer could not legally be issued without its own consent.[2] This was almost an open denial of the right of the crown and the governor to regulate the judicial system even in the slightest degree. Both parties gave evidence of considerable temper in this conflict, and Martin prorogued the assembly to March, 1774, in order to put an end to the struggle for the time.[3]

In his opening speech to the assembly of March, 1774, Martin spoke very kindly and asked the coun-

[1] C. R. IX, 707–08.
[2] C. R. IX, 737–08, 742–43.
[3] C. R. IX, 698–99, 786–87, 790–91.

cillors and representatives not to insist upon the foreign attachment clause as the indispensable provision of the bill for the regulation of courts.[1] The upper house replied that it would not make foreign attachments the only condition of its approval of such a bill.[2] But the lower house declared that the people had very cordially approved of the action of the former houses and that consequently it could not yield on attachments or its demands that it should have a share in issuing commissions of oyer and terminer.[3] On March 19 Martin gave his assent to twenty-six bills, but rejected the one for superior courts because of the provisions concerning attachment and other objectionable clauses.[4] The lower house then resolved that the possession of the right to attach the effects of foreign debtors was beneficial to the province and was founded upon equity, and that a copy of the superior court bill, which Martin had rejected, be sent to the crown.[5] While Martin and the lower house could not agree on a bill for the regulation of the superior courts, still he yielded somewhat to its demands and assented to bills for inferior courts and courts of oyer and terminer.[6] During the short session of April, 1775, one more attempt was made to secure harmony and agreement in the matter of superior courts, but the lower house still

[1] C. R. IX, 831–34.
[2] C. R. IX, 835.
[3] C. R. IX, 879–80.
[4] C. R. IX, 926–28, 862–63.
[5] C. R. IX, 939–40.
[6] C. R. IX, 946.

insisted upon the former demands and consequently no agreement was reached.[1]

Though Martin did not exercise tact in dealing with these questions, his claims were in the main legal, at least based upon his instructions from the crown while those of the lower house rested for the most part on assumptions or customs which had in the past been allowed.

Courts and judges were also the causes of conflicts between the two houses. In 1746 a bill was rejected by the upper house in consequence of no agreement being reached on the question of the extent of the jurisdiction of the inferior courts.[2] The lower house attempted to extend such jurisdiction to a very considerable degree, while the upper house asserted that such extension was contrary to the rights of the crown and, therefore, illegal. In 1756 and 1760 three court bills were rejected by the upper house because of a dispute concerning the time of holding such courts and the payment of the salaries of the justices. The lower house had by its bills fixed dates which would be very inconvenient for the chief justice and had demanded that the salaries be paid from the sinking fund instead of a poll tax; the upper house insisted upon dates which would be most convenient to the chief justice and upon the laying of a poll tax with which to pay the salaries.[3] In November, 1762, the two houses had a considerable discussion over the appointment of associate justices of

[1] C. R. IX, 988, 1190–95, 1201–11.
[2] C. R. IV, 833.
[3] C. R. V, 665–67; VI, 172–73, 175, 177, 179.

the superior courts, and especially over the issue of commissions of oyer and terminer. The upper house claimed that the king by his prerogative had the right of appointing courts of oyer and terminer, while this claim was denied by the lower house. After much dispute the lower house agreed that the governor be given the power by the legislature of issuing commissions for such courts. As this plan would deprive the crown of its right to issue such commissions independently of the lower house, the upper house would not yield and consequently rejected the bill.[1] Thus the matter dropped as far as the legislature was concerned, and it was left in the hands of the executive to provide for courts of oyer and terminer.

The two houses were in substantial agreement on judicial questions from 1763 to 1773, but during the latter year they were in conflict over the question of foreign attachments. During March, 1773, the upper house complained because the lower house had thrown out the following clause in a bill which provided for the division of the province into six districts for superior courts: "And be it further enacted that the estate of no person whatsoever, who has never resided in North Carolina, shall be liable to an attachment otherwise than by the laws and statutes of England in like cases, and that every clause and section in the before recited act shall be repealed." The lower house, while agreeing to concur with all the other suggestions of the upper house, would not permit the above clause to be inserted. It claimed that it was inconsistent with the commercial

[1] C. R. VI, 845–51, 854.

interests of the province to give up the benefit attaching the effects of those not residing in North Carolina, and that such a right was exercised by the other colonies.[1] This claim, with the rejection of the above named clause, is evidence that the lower house was demanding practical regulation of judicial matters and that it claimed rights independent of the council, governor and crown. The council would not allow the claim and rejected the bill;[2] they were willing to grant foreign attachments, provided they were according to the customs and laws of England, but beyond this they were not yet ready to go. In December of the same year this question came up again, and both houses still insisted upon their former ideas.[3] But during the March session of 1774 the upper house yielded somewhat to the demands of the lower house and a compromise was reached.[4] Prior to this the upper house had maintained the rights of the crown and governor, and was, therefore, a unit with the governor in his struggle against the encroachments of the lower house. But now the councillors were beginning to take the side of the colonists as against the crown administration, and were ready to compromise with the representatives of the people on judicial questions.

The governor and the lower house were in conflict over the questions of representation in the legislature, and what should constitute a quorum, which may be for

[1] C. R. IX, 427, 435–37.
[2] C. R. IX, 438.
[3] C. R. IX, 721–22, 726–33.
[4] C. R. IX, 844–46, 849–50, 853–54, 857.

convenience called constitutional privileges. These arose under Dobbs, Tryon and Martin; they were never critical, though at times annoying, and were never fully settled. In 1760 the lower house practically claimed that the crown had no right to compel counties and towns to take out charters of incorporation from the governor before they were entitled to representation in the legislature. Dobbs declared that this claim was contrary to the rights of the crown, and opposed to the instructions from the crown.[1] He was correct in his position, at least his declaration was backed up by specific instructions from the crown, and the lower house almost ceased to press its claim.[2] The question of the quorum was of far more importance. In 1760 Dobbs asked that the lower house act with fifteen as a quorum. It refused to do so and denied his right of determining what should constitute a quorum. It claimed that it was its own right to decide upon this; and at times it would allow twenty-five to act and again it would not make a move towards discharging business without a majority of its entire number.[3] In 1764 and 1773 it again refused to act with a quorum of fifteen as the governor asked.[4] The lower house in taking such a position was acting directly contrary to the instructions from the crown, which specifically stated that fifteen members should constitute a quorum.[5] But as this was a point of considerable importance it would not obey the

[1] C. R. VI, 245.
[2] C. R. VI, 724, 985–90; V, 1111.
[3] C. R. VI, 319–24, 344–45.
[4] C. R. VI, 1024–25; IX, 595–96.
[5] C. R. V, 1111.

crown, and would not act without a majority, or at least twenty-five, of its number. It was much more difficult for the governor to control from twenty-five to thirty-five members than fifteen; with a small quorum he might easily pass acts against the interests of the colonists it was thought, but with a large one it was almost impossible to do so.

The two houses did not dispute over representation in the legislature or what should constitute a quorum, but they did become involved in a conflict over the question of examining public claims and accounts. The chief instance of this was in 1762. The lower house appointed ten of its number as a committee on accounts, and eleven on claims, while the upper house appointed only three of its members on each. Should each house committee act separately and independently of the other in their examination of claims and accounts? It was upon this question that a dispute arose. The upper house claimed that its committees had equal rights in this with those of the lower house, though their number was by no means as large, and that its committees could act by themselves or jointly, as they liked. The lower house denied this claim, at least so far as separate and independent action was concerned.[1] If the upper house members could act only in conjunction with the lower house members, the balance of power would certainly be with the lower house, as ten or eleven to three was a very large majority. The lower house did not ask for so much power as would be given it by this arrangement, but it did demand a substantial control

[1] C. R. VI, 824–26.

in the examination of all public claims and accounts upon the ground that it represented the people who had to pay these; and this control was at several times allowed by the upper house.

We have now seen that the conflicts between the executive, the governor and council, and the lower house of the legislature arose from their different points of view on questions of land, fees, money, agent, courts and judges, and constitutional privileges. The fact has been made apparent that the governor and the council were practically a unit in their point of view and in their attempts to maintain the rights and interests of the crown; and this we should most naturally expect, as they were both the agents of the crown. The attitude of the executive toward the lower house was for the most part supported by precedents and in substantial accordance with the royal instructions; and these instructions constituted the chief guide of the executive. In some respects these were very specific, and the executive must act according to them, if possible. In other respects much was left to the interpretation and discretion of the executive. Conflicts arose between the executive and the lower house both over the specific clauses and those in the interpretation of which the executive was to use its discretion. The lower house in questioning or denying the one was attacking the policy of the crown, but in disputing over the other it was merely doubting the interpretation of the officers of the crown who resided in the province. The fact has also been made apparent that the lower house acted in sympathy with the colonists, maintaining their rights and interests. Many of their claims were not founded on a strong legal basis, but appear rather as assumptions when looked at from the purely constitutional stand-point. But there was to the minds of the colonists something greater and nobler than the English public law as applied to a royal province in the eighteenth century—the principles of freedom and independence— and during the whole of the royal period the lower house in denying the rights of the crown defended its action by appealing to these principles.

CHAPTER X.

THE DOWNFALL OF THE ROYAL GOVERNMENT.

As we have seen, the royal government of North Carolina came in most quietly, but its end was amid conflicts and disturbances of a serious kind—in revolution. It was by this revolution that the crown government went down in several other American provinces. Out of this came forth the independent states and the nation of the American people. The downfall of the crown's administration in North Carolina, as well as in the other provinces, is to be studied in the history and development of the governor, council and lower house of the legislature, and in the development of the conflicts between the executive and the lower house, the chief points of which have already been under consideration. This downfall is also to be studied in the general constitutional and commercial policies of England toward her colonies, and these will now be discussed.

We have seen that the executive and the lower house had disputes, though never of a very serious kind, over certain questions which might be called constitutional questions. These arose particularly under Dobbs, Tryon and Martin, from 1760 to 1773. Among these was whether the crown had the right to compel counties and towns to take out charters of incorporation, from the governor, before they could send delegates to the house of representatives. After some disputes over this point, the lower house practically yielded. Over the question of a quorum there was a much greater dispute, and this continued during the last fifteen years of the royal period and at its close was still unsettled. The lower house did not to any considerable degree yield its claims, that it alone had the right to decide what should constitute a quorum; it seldom allowed the number as designated by the crown to be the actual one.[1]

Along with these disputes and the conflicts arising over land, fees, money, agents, courts and judges, there was always another question; and this, though not very specific, was of fundamental importance. Underlying all of the relations of the colonists to the crown was this general question: how far do the crown's instructions to its officers in the province constitute law? The claim of the administrative boards in England and of the British officers in the colony was in the main to the effect that these instructions were to be as binding upon the colonists as if they were acts of parliament, while the colonists very frequently either questioned or denied this. In support of their position the colonists went back to the English common law, the customs of the province and their charters. These to their way of thinking made up their constitution and were more fundamental than acts of parliament, especially than the royal instructions to the governors.

[1] C. R. V, 116–7, 301–03, 352, 398, 404–07, 1111; VI, 245, 319–24, 344–45, 724, 985–90, 1024–25; IX, 595–96.

Many are the instances wherein the crown officers and the colonists took different points of view on this question—as to what really constituted their fundamental law. The former insisted rigidly upon certain instructions, while the latter frequently fell back upon "natural" justice and law, whatever these might mean. The instructions from the crown officers were as a matter of fact based largely upon the laws of England, though they were far less definite than these laws. Though less definite, still in the eyes of the crown officials they were to be just as binding upon the colonists as the acts of parliament, and at times more so.   In this respect, therefore, a difference was made between the colonists and Englishmen residing in England. To the latter the source of the government and of the laws was now parliament. By this time the really sovereign power had been taken from the king and given to the legislative body. It is true that George III. attempted to regain this for the king, but his attempts had not been fundamentally successful. Though this was true in regard to Englishmen at home, it was by no means so with the colonists. Over these the king still held much prerogative—that is he could act much more independently of parliament in his relations with the provinces than in his relations with England. Also the members of parliament were far less rigid in their interpretation of the constitution for the colonists than for Englishmen residing at home.   Public opinion in England for the most part approved of this, and practically all parties took it as a matter of fact that the colonists were subjects of England—dependents.   On the other hand the colonists claimed the same privileges, rights, and liberties as Englishmen living at home.[1]

This difference in the view point as to what constituted the fundamental law was early manifested in North Carolina, and as other elements came into conflict this was more and more strongly brought out. On this point neither side exactly understood or appreciated the other's position, and instead of coming together on it they tended farther and farther apart. This difference became very striking and important from 1763 to the end of the period. Not only was this true of North Carolina, but it was also substantially true of all the other royal provinces and to an extent of the proprietary colonies. By 1763 the idea of popular sovereignty had obtained a great hold upon many of the American colonists. Popular sovereignty as an idea had been in vogue for several years, but the personal loyalty for the king on the part of the colonists had kept it as an idea; it now became an active and living principle. This principle, coming almost simultaneously to many of the provinces, tended to unite them, and also to make the crown the less ready to yield to the demands of the colonists, as yielding in one case meant yielding in many cases. By this time the English colonists were left as masters of practically the whole of North America. The French had been conquered at the north and Florida at the south had

[1] Anson's The Law and Custom II, 32–42; Reflexions on Representation in Parliament, 1–46; Remarks on the Review of the Controversy, 1–130; North Carolina Gazette, 1773, in McRee's Iredell I, 178–80; Tyler's Literary History I, 47–52, 63–69, 70–77.

been given up by Spain. There was, therefore, no longer a great outside force to compel them to rely upon England for assistance; and besides they had discovered during the fourth intercolonial war what strength they themselves had when united. Prior to this time they had never been united, even for a short period. The colonies had been more attached to England than to one another. Similar struggles between their assemblies and the governors over land, finance, justice and other important problems, had for some time tended to bring about something of a feeling of union. It was now war, and war for a duration of more than six years, which finally united them in spirit. After its close they were still Englishmen and loyal to the English crown, but they were no longer willing to have many restraints placed upon their political freedom, which for more than a half century had been greater to the colonists than to Englishmen residing in their mother country.[1]

As has been stated, this difference of opinion as to what made up the fundamental law, according to which the colonists should in a general way be governed, was seen during the first years of the royal administration and at many different times thereafter. It was manifested upon the occasion of the disallowance or repeal by the crown of certain acts passed by the provincial assembly. The famous biennial act of 1715–1716 was disallowed in 1737, the first two royal governors advising to this effect, upon the ground of its taking away from the crown certain privileges. This was an act

[1] Lecky's History of England, III, 290–328.

15

providing for a new assembly every two years, and regulating the method of the elections and the qualifications of the electors and the representatives.[1] Both the crown and the colonists claimed that these special privileges belonged respectively to themselves. Though this act was repealed, more to substantiate the claim of the home government than for any other reason, still acts with many of the same provisions were passed and allowed in 1743, and again in 1760.[2] In 1754 twenty-six acts were repealed by the king's proclamation, and these were for the most part acts erecting counties and towns and granting them the privilege of sending representatives to the legislature.[3] This was done upon the ground that the granting of such a right belonged exclusively to the crown, not to the provincial assembly. Within two years, however, the governor was instructed to request the legislature to establish these counties and towns, provided that the right of issuing letters of incorporation to them, upon which their privilege of legislative representation depended, was reserved to the crown.[4] Five acts were disallowed by the crown in 1759, three of which erected courts of justice. These were points of fundamental importance, and both the colonists and the home government were striving after the greatest possible control over them. Acts on the same subject were repealed in 1761 and again in 1762, and for the same gen-

[1] C. R. III, 206–07; IV, 25, 251; Swann, 2; MS. Laws.
[2] Swann, 177–80; Davis, 1765, II, 198–202.
[3] C. R. V, 115–17.
[4] C. R. V, 407, 659; Davis, 1765, II, 86–88.

eral reason. During the latter part of 1762, however, acts erecting courts and defining their jurisdiction were passed and allowed, and in these acts the colonists yielded to the demands of the crown.[1] Another act erecting courts was passed in 1768–1769 with a special clause providing for the attachment of the goods of foreigners. Over this point a great constitutional battle was to be waged. This act, at least an important part of it, was deemed by the home government to be a pure assumption on the part of the provincial assembly, and Governor Martin was specially instructed to refuse his assent to any further acts containing such provisions.[2] There were several other acts which were disallowed or repealed by the crown, but most of these had involved in them no important constitutional points or results. Doubtless, however, the repeal of the act of 1771, allowing Presbyterian ministers to perform the marriage ceremony, and the repeal of the acts of the same year founding and endowing Queen's College in Mecklenburg County—a college for Presbyterians— had some influence in driving the frontier settlers away from the support of the royal government. It is certain that the Presbyterians of this county were among the first to revolt against the British colonial policy and system,[3] though exactly how far they were influenced by the repeal of these acts is not known.

With this difference in the point of view concerning certain constitutional problems went also a difference

---

[1] C. R. V, 700–02, 707, 1049.
[2] C. R. VIII, 264–65; IX, 230–36.
[3] C. R. IX, 7, 250–51, 284–85, 597, 665; Davis, 1773, 455, 480.

of opinion in regard to commercial questions and policies. During the eighteenth century, certainly until
the appearance of Adam Smith's very famous work—
"Wealth of Nations"—which came from the press in
1776, England was under the control of the mercantile
doctrines of economic thought. It was under Crom-
well as lord protector that such a policy was adopted in
England on a grand scale, and many other European
countries were then acting according to its principles.
It was in fact to become the fighting instrument of
England against Holland, a country which had for
some time been the wealthiest and greatest in commerce of all the European peoples. One of the chief
forces in giving Holland this position of supremacy had
been the mercantilist policy. The nations were now
ceasing to fight each other with the weapons of war;
their struggles were in commercial policies. During
the latter half of the seventeenth century and the first
seventy-five years of the eighteenth England was strong
and vigorous under such a policy. The eighteenth century was for England a period of great expansion; her
chief energies were now spent not at home but in carrying out her commercial and colonial policies, in North
America and Asia, in struggling for the mastery over
France, her great rival. A selfish and narrow trade
policy, one which would tend to enrich herself alone,
was, therefore, most natural, as her great expansion
demanded vast sums of money.[1]

The first decided attempt to carry out such a commer-

[1] Egerton's British Colonial Policy, 61–62; Seeley's Expansion, 9,
20; Cunningham's Eng. Industry and Commerce, Mod. Times, 256–58.

cial policy was in 1651, when the first navigation ordinance was passed. This act was for the encouragement of English shipping against that of Holland. It
did not directly work against the colonies. The act of
nine years later was intended to promote English manufacturing as well as shipping, and, therefore, brought
the provinces more closely within its influence. Now
for the first time were the mercantilist doctrines and
principles to be applied to the colonies. By the act of
1660, not only were English goods, exported or imported, to be carried in English ships exclusively, but
sugar, tobacco, cotton, wool, indigo and dye stuffs—
colonial products—were also restricted to a small market. It was forbidden that they be transported to any
places except England or another English province.[1]
Nor was this the end of such a policy. The act of
about three years later declared that no European
goods were to be transported to the provinces unless
they were first landed in England and then reëxported.[2]
England thereby received the benefits of the customs
duties and freight rates.

Such a policy, therefore, regarded the colonists as
subjects of England and to be used for the special
benefit of the mother country in enriching her and in
aiding her to triumph over her commercial and industrial rivals. From the year 1660 it had been claimed
that the very reason for the existence of the colonies
was the support which they could give England. Their
industries were under rigid regulations, based upon

[1] Egerton, 61, 68–71; 12 Charles II, c. 18.
[2] Egerton, 71–72; 15 Charles II, c. 7.

the mercantilist doctrines; the home government placed great restraints upon certain finished products and granted liberal bounties upon others—as a rule the raw products for which she had great need.[1] The colonies, therefore, must not become competitors of England, but must render her the maximum support in her ship-building, manufacturing and trading. This policy, wherein state control and interference in all kinds of economic activity were dominant ideas, was repugnant to many of the colonists, especially so when such a system was at all successfully carried out. This had much to do with creating and keeping alive the spirit of revolt and of revolution among the colonists.[2]

There is, however, little evidence of North Carolina offering protests to the general principles of this commercial policy, and none whatever to its principles as incorporated in the navigation acts. Her life during the seventeenth century was on too small a scale to be much affected by such a system. There is also comparatively little evidence of opposition to the acts of trade of the eighteenth century, as her economic activity was of such a kind as to suffer little by these, and to escape them was easy. The woolens act of 1699,[3] forbidding any woolens manufactured by the colonists to be transported to England or any other English province; the act of 1719, forbidding the colonists to make iron of any form, and the later acts[4] which substituted duties in the place of such a prohibition; the

[1] Egerton, 2.
[2] Ingram's Hist. Pol. Econ., 36–54; Marshall's Econ. I, 41; Egerton, 3; Cunningham, 332.
[3] 10 William III, c. 16.
[4] 23 George II, c. 29.

act of 1732[1] against the exportation of hats from any province; and finally the sugar act of 1733,[2] which laid a duty on all rum and spirits manufactured by other than English colonies upon their importation into any English province, and also a duty upon all sugars, molasses and syrups imported,—none of these acts of the British parliament seem to have produced any special and direct effect upon North Carolina, certainly not in alienating her from the mother country. Several of these were not well executed. North Carolina produced few of the articles included in their lists and had fine chances for smuggling.[3] Nor did the later trade acts have material effect upon the colonists of this province.

The colonists of North Carolina did, however, protest and revolt against the restrictions placed upon their issuing bills of credit, and especially against the stamp act, which placed a tax upon their business or legal transactions. As yet the home government had not levied a tax upon her provinces except in the indirect way of customs duties. But now George III., with Grenville in control of the treasury, was eager to make a great display, by a more vigorous commercial policy, by extending the power of England over her provinces and by taxing them. The system of colonial defence must be greatly improved, and this was to be done by means of the revenues from stamp taxes collected from the colonists. The great leaders of England, how-

[1] 5 George II, c. 22.
[2] 6 George II, c. 13.
[3] C. R. IV, 156, 169–72; V, 316; VI, 968, 1021–33; VII, 429; VIII, 154, 496.

ever, were by no means all in favor of this policy and method;[1] Chatham and Burke were especially opposed to them.[2] The king and Grenville proposed to have a permanent body of soldiers in the provinces, and that these be supported and supplied with provisions of war by the colonists. Though it was fair that the colonists should help in maintaining a standing army for British colonial defence, still the stamp act, whereby duties were levied with which to support such an army, was passed at a most inopportune time. The colonists themselves had rendered much assistance in defeating the French and thereby adding a vast area to the English domains. As a matter of fact, however, no one then knew that this would be the end of the struggle for the mastery of North America; perhaps the French and Indians might make further efforts at war. But it seemed to the colonists that this proposed standing army was to be used more for the purpose of aiding the English colonial customs officers, in putting an end to the smuggling which had been going on upon a great scale, than in defending the colonies against any further attacks by the Indians or French. The trade acts of 1699–1750 had been very poorly executed, and the spirit of smuggling was growing stronger. It was manifesting violence when Grenville came into power. His policy of extending England's influence, of unifying and controlling all of the provinces, and of enforcing a narrow and selfish trade system, was at once opposed by this spirit. His attempts to carry out such a policy were ill-timed and unwise. The colonists had

[1] Egerton, 178–202.
[2] Speeches, Brit. Orations.

for a long time enjoyed much self-government and practical independence; now they felt the spirit of this independence more than ever before. They had seen much evidence of their power when united against a common enemy; the fourth intercolonial war was regarded by them as a substantial victory for themselves. Prior to 1764 parliament had exercised limited control over them and now it was very difficult to make this greater and more efficient; it meant resistance. Also prior to 1750, the ministers in England had given rather little intelligent attention to the provincial affairs. Certainly Walpole and Newcastle, 1715–1750, had done so.[1] Now to carry out a different policy, to enforce all of the laws in a rigid manner, even by placing a standing army among the colonists, to tax them for its support,—all this was fundamentally different from the customs of more than a half century and was much opposed to the privileges which had been acquired during this time. So great and almost universal was the opposition of the colonists to such a plan, and especially to the stamp act, that it was repealed within a very short time after its passage. To this act North Carolina for the first time offered a serious protest, and this now in the shape of a strong and general revolt against the execution of its provisions. Hitherto her colonists had for the most part been obedient to the acts of parliament.[2]

[1] Lecky III, 328–53.

[2] Egerton, 201–02; Reflexions on Representation in Parliament, 1–46; Remarks on the Review of the Controversy, 1–30; The Necessity, etc., 1–46; Moore, the Justice and Policy of Taxing the Am. Cols., 1–16; Tyler I, 41–44, 63–69, 94–99, 101–111.

Upon the arrival of the news of the passage of the act, the people of North Carolina, as well as of the other colonies, were ready to protest and even to rebel, not so much against parliament as against the conduct of the king's ministers. This spirit of protest and revolt had more to do in uniting the colonies than any other force. The act was opposed to an extent because it meant taxes, but to a greater degree because of the principles involved. For the colonists to recognize such an act and allow it to go into effect meant a full recognition on their part of the right of parliament and of the crown officers in England not only to regulate the colonial shipping and manufacturing, as had been done in the navigation and trade acts, but also to enter their internal life, to tax, and, therefore, to regulate their private business transactions. It meant the giving up of the privileges which they had for many years enjoyed and consequently were inclined to think their own; it meant that the colonists had no rights and privileges apart from those that the parliament and the administrative bodies in England were willing to grant them; it meant that their long standing claim, that they had a constitution independent of royal instructions and parliamentary acts was to be given up forever.[1] This tax was justified on the ground that England had been to a great expense in founding and protecting the colonies and could, therefore, with justice tax them. Most probably the real reason, though not avowed, was that the home government was in very pressing need

[1] 5 George III, c. 12; C. R. VII, 123–24; Moore, The Justice and Policy of Taxing the Am. Cols., 1–16.

for more revenue, as her policy of expansion had been most expensive. On the other hand it was claimed, even by such a leader as Chatham, that the colonies had already paid for all of their founding and protection, out of their intimate and dependent trade relations with England.[1]

Whether or not the act was passed in justice, the colonists of North Carolina proceeded to acts of violence when the stamps arrived. Upon their arrival at Wilmington, the stamp master was compelled by a large crowd of people to take an oath to the effect that he would distribute none of them, and later he resigned his office. Effigies of him and of the advocates of the tax were burned in several different parts of the province, and there were other manifestations of opposition and even of violence. So great was the feeling of protest and of revolt that Governor Tryon felt called upon to use all of his diplomacy, and he was very clever in this, to keep the people from acts of great violence. He made them promises to the effect that, as they could not afford to pay such heavy taxes, he would use his best endeavors with the authorities at home for their repeal or modification.[2] The reply which was made to him by the leaders was that the colonists were still loyal to the king, but that this loyalty was that of a free, not of a dependent, people; that the act was unconstitutional and oppressive and took away rights and privileges which belonged to all Englishmen. In this they gave very decided evidence of a difference of opinion

[1] Speech, Brit. Orations; The Necessity, etc., 1–46.
[2] C. R. VII, 124–8, 130–31.

as to what made up the constitution. In fact in declaring the act unconstitutional the colonists were setting themselves up as the final interpreters of their fundamental law. Not only did they make declaration to this effect, but they also declared that nothing but a repeal of the act would relieve the situation, and that if this was not done, resistance and violence would follow. To this end a good many of the colonists took an oath.[1]

As we have seen, the stamp-master for Wilmington resigned his office, in fear of violence to himself. When the stamps arrived there on the twenty-eighth day of November, 1765, they remained on board the British sloop Diligence, as no one would take the office of stamp-master, either because of opposition to the taxes or because of the insults and perhaps violence which would come to him from his fellow citizens. The commander of the king's sloop, not being allowed to land the stamps, placed restrictions upon the shipping of the Cape Fear River, in fact forbade any ships to enter and clear until they had used the required stamps on their clearance papers. This caused another outburst of unpopular feeling against the act, especially against its execution in any manner whatever. During February of the next year a large crowd of people gathered at Brunswick, the port of Wilmington, for the purpose of condemning such restrictions upon their trade and of declaring their grievances against the ministry in England. They finally came to a compromise with the king's commander in regard to the trade hindrances. He removed all these until an investigation should be

[1] C. R. VII, 128–30.

made by the royal surveyor-general of customs. But
still the colonists were not satisfied. They compelled
the collector, naval officer and controller of customs to
take an oath to the effect that they would not attempt to
execute the stamp law until it had been accepted by the
legislature of the province, which of course would never
happen. All of this called forth Tryon's diplomatic
skill. This being used upon the chief leaders had the
effect of keeping order and preventing violent conduct.
It was, however, the repeal of the act which had most
to do in bringing about peace.[1]

When once relieved, the province continued in peace
with the crown administration until 1773, if we except
the "regulators" on the western frontier. Still the
colonists believed in their sovereign rights, especially
concerning taxes.[2] Nor was North Carolina alone in
this. Virginia and Maryland, in 1769–1770, passed certain resolves concerning the rights and powers of the
crown and of the proprietor, copies of which were sent
to the legislature of North Carolina. The Sons of
Liberty, local organizations of the colonists of South
Carolina, at about the same time, were writing letters
to the other provinces on the same topics. In these
resolves and letters one idea was very distinct—that
parliament and the ministers of the king were wholly
disregarding the real question of the provinces. This
idea had much to do in creating and fostering the spirit
of union among the colonists.[3]

[1] C. R. VII, 143, 168c-68e, 169–77, 179–99, 222–23, 232, 242–43, 877–
79, 980–82.
[2] C. R. VIII, 122–24, 170–71.
[3] C. R. VIII, 41, 158–59, 197–98.

The "regulation" troubles of 1768–1771 have already been mentioned. By most of the historians it has been asserted that they were a revolt against the crown's administration of the province, the first of the real revolutionary acts against Great Britain. But such a view is not based to any considerable extent upon the facts in the case, though it has been supported by more historical writing than almost any other event of the whole colonial period. The war of the "regulation" was an insurrection or an uprising among some of the settlers in the western counties, something of a peasants' revolt. It was not directed against the British policy and government, or even against that of Governor Tryon, but against the administration of justice and the finances by certain county officers, who were acting to a great extent for their own personal gain. The grievances of the "regulators" were high taxes, dishonest sheriffs and extortionate fees for justice, and their revolt was specifically against these, not at all against the principles of the crown's government. The fact that they had little currency with which to pay their taxes and fees added to their burdens; they were small farmers on the frontier and consequently far away from markets. Though they had an abundance with which to support themselves still their supply of money was very small.[1]

Most of the colonists were quiet and loyal to the crown for several years after the repeal of the stamp act, but still the idea and spirit of popular sovereignty were being exalted. When Governor Martin arrived

[1] C. R. VII, 718–19, 721, 887–88; VIII, 1–574, passim, 574–621; Bassett's Regulators.

in the province, during the latter part of 1771, he found this spirit very strong, though under good restraint. In fact this spirit was abroad among all of the provinces, and it was tending to bring them under one common bond. Against such a spirit Martin was to work. Though with the best of purposes and intentions he was at times quite stubborn, and he found the same disposition among many of the colonists and their representatives. His administration failed and the crown government went down in disaster under him. Most probably this would have been the case under any one as governor; the time for this seems to have come in the other colonies as well as in North Carolina. The revolutionary spirit was rife in Massachusetts and elsewhere in New England, and the colonists of the north did their utmost to stir up this spirit in the southern provinces. England, never having understood or appreciated this spirit, was also acting with much stubbornness and without much intelligent statesmanship. The mistakes of her colonial policy for a hundred years and the natural tendencies to independence among the colonists now opposed her colonial administrative system, and their combined force could not be withstood; her constitutional means of control failed and the contests were to be transferred from the administrative offices to the field of battle.

There were two important points in the final struggle in North Carolina—finances and justice. Over these Governor Martin and the lower house of the legislature had bitter and serious disputes. The chief points of these have been under consideration in another connection. Here they will be discussed only in their general bearing upon the downfall of the royal government.[1]

By the beginning of Martin's administration the finances had come to be in a very bad condition. Dobbs had left a large debt, and Tryon had added to it considerably. As we have seen, Martin and the lower house soon became involved in a dispute over special taxes connected with the sinking of a part of this indebtedness, the bills of credit issued in 1748 and 1754. The lower house, having the idea that a sufficient amount had been collected for the payment of these bills, passed an act discontinuing the taxes. Martin, having a different understanding of the fiscal status, disallowed its act. The lower house evidently expected such action on the part of the governor, and had resolved upon instructions to be sent to the collectors of taxes, to the effect that they should no longer be collected. It also indemnified any officers who might be sued by the chief executive on the grounds of disobedience or neglect.[2] Governor Martin, who perhaps had the correct idea of the situation, by proclamation ordered that the said taxes be collected. Neither party would yield its point and, therefore, no compromise could be reached. The same issue was presented again during the latter part of 1773, and with the same results.[3] Both parties claimed that they had the ulti-

[1] See Sikes, Transition, 11–14, 18–41, for a much fuller and somewhat different statement.

[2] C. R. IX, 233, 329.

[3] C. R. IX, 301, 742–43, 943–44, 954–55, 982–83; North Carolina a Royal Province, 60–61.

mate regulation of fiscal affairs. This point was so fundamentally important to each side that to yield it meant a surrender of a most vital principle. The lower house in its position was now in general agreement with its former interpretation of the constitutional law —that it was something apart from the instructions of the crown to the governors and the parliamentary acts, that it belonged to the sovereignty of the colonists. Ultimate control of the public moneys is about as great a power as that of collecting them by taxation; either one is the privilege of a sovereign body. For Martin to yield to the lower house meant a full recognition of this claim to sovereignty on the part of the colonists, and of course he was not ready to do this. Nor did the crown give up this point until the treaty of peace of 1783, after a struggle of seven years on the field of battle.

But it was upon questions of the courts and their jurisdiction that the greatest conflicts occurred, and upon these the crown government went down in disaster. Justice, as well as the finances, is very closely connected with the real life of any body politic; the judicial and fiscal systems are the great foundation stones of any province or state. But the system of justice in the province of North Carolina had a rather unstable existence, in spite of its vital importance. The laws for the erection of courts were rarely for longer periods than two years, and these laws the governor could reject and the crown disallow or repeal. Consequently questions of the administration of justice were very frequently before the assembly and almost

16

as frequently under contention between the executive and the representatives of the colonists. As we have seen, these became of very absorbing interest under Governor Martin. When he arrived the system of 1768 was in operation, and this was in many respects like the former ones, though it was for five years' duration. The act which provided for this contained a clause concerning foreign attachments which, though at the time of passage received little consideration, was afterwards to become the subject of a great struggle— a veritable rock upon which the royal government went to pieces.[1]

In the assembly of the early part of 1773 a bill was introduced for the renewal of the system, mainly upon the same lines as those of the act of five years earlier. Now the clause providing for the attachment of the goods of foreigners became at once the bone of great contention, as it was contrary to the crown's instructions.[2] By these instructions the province was allowed only those privileges of attachment which were established by the laws of England in similar cases. The larger English towns had long had the custom of attaching the goods or debts of a debtor in the hands of a third party, having this privilege not by the laws of England—that is by acts of parliament—but by grants of the kings issued to them; it had been their only means of securing the payment of debts due from foreign merchants.[3] It should be stated that this privi-

[1] C. R. IX, 373.

[2] C. R. IX, 235–36, 378; Martin II, 294.

[3] Bohun, *Privilegia Londoni*, 252–55; also Locke, Foreign Attachments, 19.

lege did not exist by the laws of England strictly speaking, and to grant to North Carolina only those privileges provided for in these laws was to grant very little. The province could not by such a plan enjoy any right of foreign attachment worth consideration. The king in his instructions to Governor Martin was not, therefore, allowing the colonists by any means the same privileges as the commercial towns of England had for a long time enjoyed. In the struggle which went on in the legislature over this point the upper house at first was opposed to the claims of the lower house, but later it yielded to the extent of signing an act providing for the attachment of the goods of foreigners, as far as was allowed in England, provided that it contain a clause suspending its execution until the crown expressed its opinion upon the point at issue.[1] The governor, mainly to bring the matter before the law officers at home, gave his assent, but this act was soon disallowed by the king in council, and upon the advice of the crown lawyers.[2] This was unmistakable evidence that the crown would not yield to the demands of the colonists.

Pending this decision the province must have courts of some kind, and the matter of providing them for the time was at once taken up. The conflicts again became strong and bitter; nothing was accomplished and the assembly was dissolved.[3] The colony was now left without any general courts. Only the minor courts of magistrates were in operation, and these were very lim-

[1] C. R. IX, 436, 558–60.
[2] C. R. IX, 670.
[3] C. R. IX, 534, 578–79, 581, 587, 595–96, 619–32.

ited in their jurisdiction. Crimes and offences went unpunished and consequently became more frequent.[1] To relieve this situation the governor issued commissions of oyer and terminer for the trial of the criminals then in the prisons, but this action at once became the subject of much discussion by the leaders of the opposition and became another item of opposition to the crown administration.[2] When the new assembly—and there were many of the members of the former one in it—met in December, 1773, the situation had changed very little. While the upper house was still largely in favor of the crown's instructions concerning the question of foreign attachments, the lower house was more determined to carry its point; its members declared that their conduct had been strongly approved by their constituents.[3] They not only refused to compromise with the governor—and in this their spirit of independence was very decided and strong—but they also appointed a standing committee of correspondence which should keep in close touch with similar committees in the other provinces and especially keep well informed in regard to every act of the British government. For this, as well as for their very vigorous opposition to his requests, Governor Martin prorogued the assembly. Nothing had been accomplished during a session of seventeen days, and the province was again left without courts and with all the consequences attending such a

[1] C. R. IX, 625, 686.
[2] C. R. IX, 686–87, 699–706.
[3] C. R. IX, 711, 729, 738, 742–43.

condition.[1]   Peace and order were to be preserved only at the will of the colonists.

At the next meeting of the legislature, early in the next year, the same problem again presented itself, and, as the disposition of the lower house was still unchanged, again nothing could be accomplished concerning an act for erecting superior courts. The upper house was now beginning to take sides with the representatives of the people. Though no compromise could be reached upon superior courts, the attachment clause being the reason for the failure, still both parties came to an agreement upon acts providing for inferior courts of pleas and quarter sessions and also for sessions of oyer and terminer. The province was, therefore, again to have the benefits of a system of justice, though very incomplete.[2]   The assembly was now prorogued to the 25th of May, but it did not meet again at that time, as Governor Martin saw no hope of its accomplishing any results which would be beneficial to the crown. His delay in calling it into session was severely denounced by many of the political leaders. They were very anxious to have another opportunity of opposing his administration and of declaring their grievances against the king's ministers. The situation was now very grave; the province had no superior courts and the commissions of oyer and terminer issued by the last legislature were faulty. Another meeting

[1] C. R. IX, 707, 779, 786–87, 791.
[2] C. R. IX, 831–35, 862–63, 870–72, 879–80, 945–47, 966, 1009.

of the assembly must be held or the people would call a convention of themselves.[1]

Not only in North Carolina, but also in all of the other colonies, there was now much agitation, and this was very strong and revolutionary in Massachusetts. This province in its conduct had been most offensive to the home government, and it was now to be made an example in the punishment inflicted for such a conduct. In 1774 its chief port was declared closed, its charter modified, losing thereby some of its privileges and rights, and its citizens were to be sent to England for trial when under the indictment of murder or other capital offences.[2] This was the vigorous way in which the home government proposed to punish a rebellious province, and the effects of such action on the part of the crown were far different than had been expected; it had a wonderful influence in uniting the colonies into one common idea and spirit of opposition and defence. Now the idea of popular sovereignty, which had been gradually developing in the different provinces, through constitutional struggles, was to become the absorbing principle not only of each province but also of the newly created entity—the American spirit. The Americans were now to be reckoned with. In the past it had been the colonists, and with many different views, that England had to deal with. And these Americans now, fearing that a military despotism was rapidly

[1] C. R. IX, 950, 968–69; Jones 99, 124; McRee's Iredell I, 193–217.
[2] Egerton, 218; 14 George III, c. 19; 14 George III, c. 45; 14 George III, C. 39; C. R. IX, 983–94.

coming upon them, were determined to struggle for their liberties, even unto death.[1]

In North Carolina there was much of this same feeling and spirit. As Governor Martin did not call the assembly into session in May, 1774, according to the prorogation, the Whig leaders demanded a convention of the people which should take under consideration the situation of the province and also send delegates to the proposed continental congress; and in this they were acting upon the suggestion of the committee of correspondence of Massachusetts. A meeting of the citizens of Wilmington was held during July of this year, at which a call for a congress to take the place of the assembly, which the royal governor would not allow to meet, was issued. This meeting also declared in favor of a general continental congress, in which all the points at issue between the colonies and the English government should be discussed.[2] In other places similar meetings were held and with the same results. A provincial congress must be called into session in which the colonists from all parts of the province could have a voice; and such a congress was held on the 25th of August of this year. The people were alarmed and were ready to act, even in violence. There were practically no courts of justice and no assembly, and there was also little prospect of a change on the part of Governor Martin.[3] Not only was this congress, though wholly a revolutionary body, called, but the committees

[1] McRee's Iredell I, 193–220, 245–54.
[2] C. R. IX, 1016–17; McRee's Iredell I, 193–94.
[3] C. R. IX, 1025–41.

of correspondence became committees of safety also; they assumed control of the local administration in many places. In short the whole province, as well as many of its counties, was assuming independence of the crown's administration, though it was openly professing allegiance to the king.[1]

The congress, with representatives from thirty-six of the forty-four counties, met in Newbern at the appointed time in spite of the governor's proclamation to the contrary. It elected a presiding officer, John Harvey, considered letters from the committees of correspondence of several of the colonies, appointed three delegates—Hooper, Hewes and Caswell—to represent the province at the continental congress to be held during September in Philadelphia, passed many resolves, among which were those supporting the house of Hanover upon the English throne. It declared fidelity to the crown but swore a hostile opposition to many of its ministers, and finally announced that unless the grievances were redressed by the first of October, 1775, all commercial relations between Great Britain and North Carolina would cease. Having done this much, and also having arranged for another meeting of the congress, it adjourned;[2] and this was a very decided step towards open revolt.

Nor were the colonists, especially the Whig leaders, to stop here with their revolutionary proceedings. In

[1] C. R. IX, 1050–61, 1073–75, 1079–81, 1088–91, 1095, 1098–1113; X, 63–64, 116; The Proceedings of the Safety Committee for the Town of Wilmington, 1–76, passim.

[2] C. R. IX, 1041–49.

February of the next year a call was issued for a new provincial congress to be held in April, mainly for the purpose of electing delegates to a second continental congress. This congress, having delegates from thirty-three of forty-four counties, met at Newbern on April 3, notwithstanding the governor's proclamation against such conduct, and at the same time and place as the meeting of the assembly which Martin had again called into session. John Harvey was both speaker of the lower house of the legislature and the presiding officer of the congress—a very strange situation.[1] To a long speech made by Governor Martin on the critical conditions of the colonies and in denunciation of such irregular proceedings as the two provincial congresses in North Carolina and the one continental congress in Philadelphia, the lower house replied by declaring in favor of these bodies and by avowing its sympathy and support for the cause of Boston as being the common cause of all the American colonists. After four days' session without accomplishing any results the assembly was dissolved, and this was the last legislature under the crown. The congress, which was by this time the real governing body in the province, expressed its approval in unqualified terms of the work of the first continental congress, appointed delegates to a second, and instructed their presiding officer to call another provincial congress in case of need.[2]

Governor Martin now realized that his control was gone and, therefore, began to look to his own protection;

[1] C. R. IX, 1108, 1126, 1145–46, 1177–79, 1185, 1187, 1204.
[2] C. R. IX, 1178–85, 1190–96, 1201–05, 1201–05, 1212.

250 NORTH CAROLINA

he was not only closely watched by the committee of
safety of Newbern but his letters also were intercepted
by them. In May he escaped from Newbern to Fort
Johnston, at the mouth of the Cape Fear River, in
search of greater security, and soon went aboard his
majesty's sloop Cruizer, which was stationed there.[1]
From the time of his flight from Newbern there was no
longer a royal governor or administration in North
Carolina; the crown's government had indeed been
overthrown, never again to be restored. About this
time Mecklenburg County on the western frontier drew
up decidedly strong declarations of rights and practical
independence of Great Britain, and within a month of
this New Hanover and Cumberland, two counties in
the southeastern part of the province, took a more radical step organizing associations for the purpose of resisting the mother country by force of arms. In the
meantime the committees of safety in practically all of
the counties assumed control and administered the local
affairs.[2] But there was great need of a general government over all of the province; the colonists must
now organize a provincial or state administrative system with its executive, legislative and judicial departments, one which could take the place of the royal government which they had just set aside. This was to be
accomplished in part by a third provincial congress,
having in it representatives from every district, which

[1] C. R. IX, 1215, 1254–58; X, 1–69, 74–75, 69–71, 96–98, 141–51.
[2] C. R. X, 9–12, 14–15, 20–30, 83, 87–93, 99–100, 105, 112–16, 120–22,
134–37, 139–41, 151–52, 157–64; Proceedings of the Safety Committee
for the Town of Wilmington, 1–76.

met at Hillsboro on the 25th of August.[1] When this body met a wholly new work was presented to it, not one of tearing down an old system, as had been the case with the first two congresses, but of reorganization and the building up of a new one. With its meeting this chapter comes to a close. The royal government had fallen.

[1] C. R. X, 141, 164–220.

BIBLIOGRAPHY.

Inasmuch as this study is based almost entirely upon the sources, a comparatively small number of works will be included in the bibliography. However, every treatise which in any way deals with the subject, directly or indirectly, has been examined and considered. Not only have the collections in North Carolina and New York City, dealing with the provincial life of North Carolina, been investigated, but most of the important works dealing with the other American colonies have also been under consideration.

FIRST-HAND SOURCES ON NORTH CAROLINA.

PRINTED.

The Colonial Records of North Carolina; 10v.; 1886–1890.
The State Records of North Carolina; 10v.; 1895–1902.
The Swann Revisal of North Carolina Statutes; 1v.; 1751–1752.
The Davis Revisal of North Carolina Statutes; 2v.; 1764–1765.
The Davis Revisal of North Carolina Statutes; 1v.; 1773.
The Iredell Revisal of North Carolina Statutes; 1v.; 1791.

MANUSCRIPT.

Laws of North Carolina, 1715–1774, at intervals; these give in full
    several of the acts which the Revisals have only by title.
Land Warrants.
Land Surveys.
Records of Land Grants.
The Granville MS. Warrants, Indentures and Surveys.

OTHER FIRST-HAND SOURCES.

The Statutes at Large of England; 105v.; v. 14–28; 1762–1865.
The Statutes of the Realm of England; 9–10 v.; 1810–1828.
HENING, W. W.—Statutes at Large of Virginia; 13v.; 1823.

The New Annual Register; 1791.
The Proceedings of the Safety Committee of the Town of Wilmington,
North Carolina, 1774–1776; 1844.
BANCROFT, E.—Remarks on the Review of the Controversy between
Great Britain and her Colonies; 1769, London; 1771, New Lon-
don in New England.
MOORE, M.—The Justice and Policy of Taxing the American Colonies
in Great Britain, Considered; 1765, Wilmington, N. C.
The Necessity, etc.; 1765–1766; Author unknown.
POWNALL, T.—The Administration of the Colonies; 4 ed., 1768.
Reflexions on Representation in Parliament; 1766, London; Author un-
known.
STOKES, A.—A View of the Constitution of the British Colonies in
North America and the West Indies; 1783.

SECOND–HAND WORKS.

ANSON, W. R.—The Law and Custom of the Constitution; 2v.; 1896.
BASSETT, J. S.—The Constitutional Beginnings in North Carolina; J.
H. U. Studies, v. 12; 1894.
BASSETT, J. S.—Landholding in Colonial North Carolina; T. C. His-
torical Papers, Series II.; 1898.
BASSETT, J. S.—The Regulators of North Carolina; A. H. A. Reports;
1894.
BATTLE, K. P.—History of the Supreme Court of North Carolina; 1889.
BEER, G. L.—The Commercial Policy of England toward the American
Colonies; 1893.
BOHUN, W.—*Privilegia Londoni;* 1702.
BRICKELL, John—The Natural History of North Carolina; 1737.
BULLOCK, C. J.—Essays on the Monetary History of the United States;
1901.
CARUTHERS, E. W.—The Life of Doctor David Caldwell; 1842.
CHALMERS, George—An Introduction to the History of the Revolt of
the American Colonies; 2v.; 1845.
CHALMERS, George—Opinions of Eminent Lawyers on English Juris-
prudence, Chiefly on the Colonies; 1858.
CUNNINGHAM, W.—The Growth of English Industry and Commerce,
Modern Times; 1892.
DOYLE, J. A.—The English Colonies in North America; 3v.; 1882–1887.

EGERTON, H. E.—A Short History of the British Colonial Policy; 1897.

FOOTE, W. H.—Sketches of North Carolina; 1846.

GNEIST, Rudolf—History of the English Constitution; 2v.; 1896.

GNEIST, Rudolf—History of the English Parliament; 1895.

GREENE, E. B.—The Provincial Governor in the English Colonies of North America; 1898.

HAWKS, F. L.—History of North Carolina, 1584–1729; 2v.; 1857–1858.

INGRAM, J. K.—A History of Political Economy; 1888.

JONES, J. S.—A Defence of the Revolutionary History of the State of North Carolina; 1834.

LECKY, W. E. H.—The History of England in the Eighteenth Century; 8v.; 1888–1891.

LORD, E. L.—Industrial Experiments in the British Colonies; 1896.

McCRADY, E.—The History of South Carolina under the Proprietary Government; 1897.

McCRADY, E.—The History of South Carolina under the Royal Government; 1899.

McREE, G. J.—Life and Correspondence of James Iredell; 2v.; 1857.

MARSHALL, A.—Principles of Economics; v. 1; 1898.

MARTIN, F. X.—The History of North Carolina, to 1776; 2v.; 1829.

MILLS, R.—Statistics of South Carolina; Charleston, S. C.; 1826.

RAPER, C. L.—North Carolina a Royal Province; 1901.

RAPER, C. L.—The Church and Private Schools of North Carolina; 1898.

SEELEY, J. R.—The Expansion of England; 1888.

SEELEY, J. R.—The Growth of the British Policy; 2v.; 1895.

SELIGMANN, E. R. A.—Essays in Taxation, 3rd ed.; 1900.

SIKES, E. W.—The Transition of North Carolina from Colony to Commonwealth; 1898.

TYLER, M. C.—The Literary History of the American Revolution; v. 1 (1763–1776); 1897.

VAN TYNE, C. H.—The Loyalists in the American Revolution; 1902.

WADDELL, A. M.—A Colonial Officer and His Times; 1890.

WEEKS, S. B.—The Religious Development in the Province of North Carolina; 1892.

WEEKS, S. B.—The Church and State in North Carolina; 1893.

WEEKS, S. B.—The Press of North Carolina in the 18th Century; 1891.

WEEKS, S. B.—A Bibliography of the Historical Literature of North Carolina; 1895.

WILLIAMSON, H.—The History of North Carolina; 2v.; 1812.

INDEX.

17